For You The War Is Over

Ian Mather

For You The War Is Over

Published by Ian Mather, 7 Grand Avenue, Muswell Hill, London N10 3AY

Book Design and Layout by Brian Price

First published 2010

Printed in 2014 by Berforts Information Press, The Old School House, Castle Rising, King's Lynn, Norfolk, PE31 6AG, United Kingdom

ISBN Number 978-0-9567612-0-0

To Katie, Roderick, Juliet, and especially Margaret, without whom nothing would have been possible.

Argentina and The Falklands

Introduction

If the first duty of a good reporter is to be in the right place at the right time, then it could be argued that there was one occasion when I failed utterly. As the result of being in the wrong place at the wrong time I found myself in a situation which few would envy: a prisoner in enemy territory. During the Falklands War between the United Kingdom and Argentina in 1982 I was arrested in Argentina, charged with espionage and locked up. I was not in just any prison. It was the most southerly in the world, on the edge of Antarctica in the Antarctic winter. Worse than the freezing cold, however, was the fact that I was in the hands of Argentine Naval Intelligence. This was the arm of the state that had been mainly responsible for the worst atrocities of the "Dirty War" that had started around 1976 following a military coup that had brought the three-man military Junta to power. Thousands of people, so-called "subversives", had been snatched and their bodies never found. Though the worst of it was over it did not in fact end until the following year, 1983. I will always maintain that I was only doing my job, but the truth is that if as a journalist you are working in a country that is at war with your own country you cannot escape the fact that you are a citizen of the enemy. Worse, you are likely to be perceived as being an agent of the enemy, especially by governments that do not understand the concept of an independent press. In my case, The Observer, of which I was Defence Correspondent, was critical of the war, a fact that I repeatedly tried to point out to my captors. It was not even taken into consideration when the Argentine prosecutors mounted their espionage case against me.

Even so, looking back I now realise that this was an experience I am glad I had. I would certainly not want to repeat it. It was frightening at times, and I simply did not know whether I would emerge alive. But I did have an extraordinary angle on the Falklands War, viewed entirely through the bars of a prison cell in Argentina. As time has gone by I have also come to appreciate that the experience of having "done time" with members of the criminal class of Tierra Del Fuego, an area known as "the uttermost part of the earth", while a war between our two countries raged nearby, is unique. In that sense, my assignment in Argentina was not a failure at all. For years I resisted pressure from my family to tell this story in detail, arguing that I was too busy. That I have finally succumbed is due to the credit crunch, which, by depriving me of my remaining journalistic and other paid activities that have kept me busy in retirement, has removed that excuse. So this book is written primarily at their behest and for them. I hope it is of interest to others too, and if that it so it is a bonus for which I am grateful.

Model of prisoner in old Ushuaia prison, now a museum

The author's cell in the present-day prison

CHAPTER ONE

BACKGROUND

I have been asked on more than one occasion "Have you ever broken into a house, and then claimed you smelt gas?" . The question reflects not only the low opinion in which journalists are held – down at the bottom of the league table along with politicians and estate agents - but also the common perception that journalists will do anything, even break the law, in order to get a story. At the opposite extreme, is the journalists' memorial at Bayeux in Normandy, where there are inscribed the names of over 2,000 journalists killed while doing their job, a total which is rising all the time, and which includes a number of friends of mine. Journalism is a hugely diverse profession embracing rogues and heroes, with the vast majority of us residing somewhere in the middle. Journalists do not work to public service regulations, nor do they have the time scale that academics enjoy in coming to considered judgements. Everything has to be done now. It is fast-moving, brutally competitive, and relatively open in that if we make mistakes they are on display the next day for all to read. That fine Sunday Times reporter, Nicholas Tomalin, famously wrote: "the only qualities essential for real success in journalism are rat-like cunning, a plausible manner and a little literary ability." I agree, although why rats, I'm not sure. This sort of behaviour is encouraged by news editors, who rarely concern themselves with the niceties of how a story has been obtained. News editors themselves are under just as much pressure from their editors to get results from their reporters, and so in turn are editors who are answerable to proprietors who want to sell more newspapers in order to make more money - or to lose less money in some cases. Newspapers belong firmly in the market place, and are a classic example of capitalism red in tooth and claw. The justification for all this, of course, is that a little white lie here and there is a small price to pay for the noble cause of bringing vital information into the public arena. In other words, the end justifies the means. That newspapers do play a vital role in a democracy is undoubtedly true. But there is also a huge element of hypocritical humbug. A lot of what is printed is just tittle-tattle, and the much-trumpeted defence that publication is in the public interest is more likely to mean that it is of interest to the public, and that can often be trivial, even prurient.

At the tabloid end of the market there may be the odd rogue who would break into houses, though I do not know any. As we learned from a recent court case that resulted in the News of the World's Royal Correspondent going to prison, there are those who break into people's privacy by hacking into their phones. I would never dream of doing either of these things myself. Neither have I ever donned a white coat and gone into a hospital pretending to be a doctor in order to secure an interview with a famous patient. But before you condemn such a practice consider the case of Farzad Bazoft. Farzad was a young Iranian journalist desperate to break into British journalism. He managed to secure a freelance arrangement with The Observer and sat at the desk next to mine at the office, where he began to specialise in Middle East stories, usually asking me to polish them up for him. He bought a flat near us in Muswell Hill, North London, visited us regularly and followed my work closely. One day just after I happened to mention to him that The Observer had rejected the offer of a free flight from the Iraqi embassy to observe some (highly dubious) elections in Saddam Hussein's Iraq he disappeared. The next we heard was that he had been arrested in Iraq. He had taken up the Iraqi embassy's offer on his own initiative. Once in Baghdad he had met up with an English nurse who worked there and after putting on white coats they had managed to penetrate a secret military complex near al-Iskandariya 25 miles south of

Baghdad where there had been reports of a mysterious explosion. He took photographs, made notes, drew drawings, picked up samples of soil and an old shoe, and returned to Baghdad. He was arrested and put on trial. The Observer did everything it could to save him, but as an Iranian in the aftermath of a long and bitter war between Iraq and Iran he stood no chance. He was convicted of spying for Israel and hanged on 15 March 1990. He is buried in Highgate cemetery and his name is on the journalists' memorial in Bayeux. Was he wrong to don that white coat? Foolish to the point of madness, yes. But unethical, surely not. After all, he might have uncovered information that Saddam Hussein was developing chemical, biological or nuclear weapons. Then no one would have asked how he came about the information. After the overthrow of Saddam Hussein it was in fact discovered that the explosion at the site had been caused by a crude attempt to make an atomic bomb.

Journalists in general consider that they have some sort of special licence to do whatever is necessary to be first with the news. The same mind set of being somehow above the law, or at least beyond the reach of "petty regulations" applies to foreign correspondents as well, though I would contend that on the whole they have greater justification. On the more upmarket newspapers at least, foreign news is taken seriously. To send reporters around the world is expensive, yet it rarely sells newspapers. Newspapers do it because they take their obligations seriously. Having committed themselves to a considerable outlay they expect their foreign correspondents to be ruthless in pursuit of the story and to take personal risks. Those who wait for a tour of the battlefield organised by the Information Ministry may wait for ever. Those who set off on their own and try to bribe, blag or bully their way to the battle zone are much more likely to come back with the story. But they may end up dead. Another of those whose names are engraved in stone at Bayeux is that of Tomalin, author of the classic quote above, who was killed when his car was hit by a rocket near the front line between Israel and Syria in the Yom Kippur War in 1973.

In 1982, the year in which the events in which I became caught up took place, newspapers had still not surrendered to television, and still considered themselves the primary vehicle for news, both domestic and foreign. Even the popular newspapers had large staffs overseas. I remember seeing a photograph in the UK Press Gazette, the house magazine of journalism, showing the foreign news team of the Daily Express. It included their foreign-based correspondents and the London-based foreign news desk staff, with the foreign editor sitting in the middle of the front row like a football manager. The reason I remember it so well is that there were 22 people on the photo, enough for two football teams. The Express, Mail and even the Mirror had full-time staff reporters in major cities around the world, all on full salaries, expenses and allowances, which even included public school fees. Today the three papers do not have a single staff foreign correspondent among them. There was intense competition among newspapers, and all reporters were required to carry their passports with them at all times, as they could be sent anywhere in the world at no notice whatsoever. I once left home for the office in my working suit, and did not return for several weeks, having been sent to Africa. I came back with a complete new set of clothes, including the suitcase in which I carried them. Reporters were issued with "air travel cards". Mine permitted me to purchase unlimited air travel on any airline, including first class, and even to charter aircraft, which I did a number of times.

With the stakes so high and the competition so ferocious it should come as no surprise that foreign correspondents considered that the odd breach of regulations was entirely justified. Bribing one's way past road blocks in Third World Countries, with either money or packets of cigarettes, was par for the course. For some reason I have never understood, Park cigarettes remain the favoured international currency for negotiating road blocks all over the world. For foreign correspondents the equivalent of breaking into a house is breaking into a country. When a war or revolution breaks out many governments, especially non-democratic ones, are highly sensitive to the presence of foreign journalists, whom they cannot control as easily they can control their domestic journalists by threatening to have them sacked, imprisoned or even worse. They want to restrict access to sensitive areas, and they view with special suspicion those foreign correspondents from wealthy countries who descend on them in times of crisis, and then set about using their financial muscle to try to reach "hot spots" that the governments don't want the world to see. So they have a habit of refusing entry to journalists until a time of their own choosing, which means when they are winning or have brought a chaotic situation under control. This is exactly the opposite of what journalists want, which is to get close to the action and get the story back to their newspapers as quickly as possible.

As a consequence, foreign correspondents developed a few of their own tricks of the trade. An obvious one was "accidentally" to leave a 100 dollar bill between the pages of one's passport when handing it to an immigration official. But that could be extremely risky, as the result could be time spent in an extremely unpleasant Third World prison, with the correspondent not being allowed to leave until after being relieved of even more funds. British passports used to state the holder's profession, which was a great inconvenience. American passports did not, and American reporters were the envy of their British colleagues as they glided effortlessly through border controls. Among British foreign correspondents the practice grew up of changing the profession shown on the passport in a way that was economical with the truth but not downright dishonest. Some foreign correspondents described themselves as "writer", which was accurate since journalists write words, and had the virtue of avoiding the dreaded word "journalist". "author" was another favoured occupation, again perfectly true. A third was "representative", true but completely meaningless with the disadvantage that it invited the obvious question: "What or whom do you represent?" One or two described themselves as "director", on what grounds I don't remember, but it had the advantage of making the passport-holder seem important, always an advantage when dealing with immigration officials. Clare Hollingworth, the magnificent foreign correspondent of the Daily Telegraph for many years, now living in Hong Kong and still going strong at the age of 99 at the time of writing, had her own solution. She managed to keep the "occupation" space blank. "What is your occupation, Madam", she was asked at Cairo airport. "What do you mean?" she demanded imperiously. "Work, Madam. What is you work?" "Work!" she bellowed in her best Lady Bracknell voice. "Are you suggesting I work? How dare you?" She was allowed in.

Television news teams with all their equipment packed in huge metal boxes never had much of a choice compared with print journalists equipped with little more than notebook, biro and either a typewriter in days gone by or a laptop nowadays. I was lucky enough to slip unnoticed into Afghanistan immediately after the Soviet invasion in 1979, one of the first Western journalists to do so. I could not help but be amused at the travails of some of my colleagues as journalists were turned away in droves. At Kabul airport I watched a heroic effort by one US TV reporter who was determined to file at least one report from Afghan soil. He started his "into camera" piece while he and his crew were walking down the aircraft steps. "Well, here we are in Afghanistan," he declared to the camera. "And over there are the Russians. You can't see them. I can't see them. But they're down that road. And we're going to go down that road, and we're going to find the Russians!" Oh no, they were not! His shoes had hardly touched the ground when he and his crew were surrounded by Afghan officials and bundled back up the steps of the plane, which was due to leave for Delhi. That was all they saw of Afghanistan.

In 1968 I officially became a "researcher", according to my passport. It came about as the result of the Soviet invasion of Czechoslovakia. The Foreign Office was desperate to find out what was happening in the country after more than 175,000 Soviet and Warsaw Pact troops marched in on the night of 20-21 August 1968 to snuff out the liberalising communist regime known as "socialism with a human face", which the Czechoslovak Government had embraced. The Kremlin saw the Czechoslovak leader, Alexander

Dubcek, and his colleagues as a grave threat to its iron-fisted grip on Eastern Europe, and ordered the borders to be sealed against Western journalists. At the Czechoslovak-Austrian border, where I and others were attempting to enter Czechoslovakia, there was a daily charade, which was being repeated at other crossing points from the West. Journalists would approach the border in the hope of being given a visa, only to be turned away when the immigration officials looked inside their passports. The next step was to wait until there was a shift change, and then try again. After repeated attempts some correspondents were lucky enough to come across a border official who was less beady-eyed, and so managed to get into the country. Some used their ingenuity. There was a memorable scene when Colin Lawson, a veteran Daily Express correspondent based in the West German capital, Bonn, was seen touring his colleagues. "Anyone got a black biro?" he asked. When he eventually procured one he used it to change the "r" in "writer" on his passport to an "a", and so entered Czechoslovakia as a waiter.

Another course of action was to return to London and apply for a new passport, which is what I did. I chose "researcher" because the Daily Mail, for whom I then worked did have researchers, whose job was to assist journalists, I thought it might be useful to have an occupation that immigration officials would not recognise as a pseudonym for journalism. When Syria invaded Jordan in September 1970 to assist the Palestinians, who were at war with the official Jordanian army of King Hussein I took a taxi from Beirut to the Syrian border, presented my passport at the border post and asked for a visa. "What is this researcher?" the official asked. I remembered the Ideal Home Exhibition at Olympia which was an annual event sponsored by the Daily Mail. "My company organises exhibitions of new homes," I replied truthfully but irrelevantly. "Ah, economist", he replied. I was unsure whether it was supposed to be a question, but my silence was enough. He stamped a visa in my passport, and I was in. I was the only journalist in the world to witness Syrian tanks racing across the desert into Jordan. I have even stamped a visa in my

17

passport when an official was not looking. In February 1979 when I and two German colleagues were desperate to drive up the Khyber Pass from Pakistan into Afghanistan before darkness fell to cover the story of the murder of the American ambassador in Kabul, we crept round the counter at the Afghan consulate in Peshawar and stamped our passports with a visa stamp that lay conveniently nearby while through a half open door we could see the consul in a back room having lunch with his family. I decided to remain officially a researcher each time I renewed my passport until eventually the requirement to state your occupation was abolished.

In my own defence I should stress that this and similar practices, which were common among newspaper foreign correspondents in my heyday, were intended only to find a way of finding out what was going on, which is the very essence of reporting. Of course, giving wrong information and tampering with passports are criminal offences. But journalists have always managed to convince themselves that they have some sort of unofficial special licence to break the rules in their never-ending chasing after stories. They accept that what they do is technically wrong, but consider that all it mounts to are mildly reprehensible misdemeanours that are likely to lead to nothing more than a summons to the Information Ministry for a metaphorical rap across the knuckles, or in more serious cases the confiscation of notebooks or camera film and expulsion from the country. Moreover, expulsion is a badge of honour for a journalist, and results in dramatic headlines, which reflect favourably on the journalist and unfavourably on the government concerned. That actually happened to me in January 1969, when I was finally expelled from Czechoslovakia by the Russians for "inflammatory" reports. Having struggled for several weeks to get more than a few paragraphs a day in the paper from Prague I finally got my picture on the front page above a story with the headline: "Czechs expel Mail Man", and also a huge feature article I had written earlier that had not been used, plus a news story.

Another hazard facing foreign correspondents is relevant to

the narrative that follows. It comes from governments themselves. Just as genuine foreign correspondents often pretend to a different occupation to get into countries, so governments use the profession of journalism as a cover for their agents. In the course of a long career I have come to know several journalists who in reality were agents of the British government, and one or two who were agents of foreign governments. There must have been others I met who succeeded in keeping their true role secret. Journalism is an ideal cover for espionage since a press pass gives its holder the freedom to go anywhere and talk to anyone at every level of society without arousing suspicion. At The Observer there were journalists who had worked for MI6 previously and possibly were still doing so when I was employed there. In the past the newspaper's proprietor and editor, David Astor, had had a standing arrangement with the Foreign Office whereby the FO and The Observer shared the costs of certain individuals, thus saving both organisations money in salaries and expenses. This arrangement went spectacularly wrong with Kim Philby, a high-ranking member of British intelligence, who was the correspondent in Beirut for The Observer and The Economist. In 1963 he fled to Russia when on the point of being outed as a double agent. All along he had been an operative for the KGB, and after he arrived in Moscow he was made a Hero of the Soviet Union in recognition of his endeavours. Because governments were accustomed to using journalism as a convenient cover for their agents they had a natural propensity to suspect other countries' journalists of being spies. Thus the abuse of journalism by governments puts all genuine foreign correspondents at risk. I was to discover this to my cost.

However, I do not want to be thought of as a victim. Far from it. I arrived in Argentina with the mind set of an experienced foreign correspondent with decades of travel for the Daily Mail and then The Observer behind me. Like all my colleagues I was prepared to take any reasonable risk to find the best stories. I had no need to try to enter the country illicitly since Argentina like other Latin American countries did not require visas for British citizens. Moreover, beneath the protective umbrella of an internationally respected newspaper I assumed that the worst that could happen if I fell foul of the Argentine authorities would be a reprimand, and possibly expulsion. I could not have been more wrong. For this time things were different. For the first time in my career I was a citizen of the enemy.

CHAPTER TWO

INTO THE DANGER ZONE

When Argentina invaded the Falkland Islands, which lie 300 miles off its coast, in April 1982 few thought it would lead to war. The United States was the most powerful player in Latin America, and the Administration of Ronald Reagan threw all its resources into trying to negotiate a settlement between Britain and Argentina. In Britain amidst a frenzy of military activity Prime Minister Margaret Thatcher despatched a naval task force. But the fact that it would take three weeks to sail the 8,000 miles to the South Atlantic was widely seen as an opportunity for diplomacy to do its work. The US Secretary of State, Alexander Haig, began to shuttle backwards and forwards between London and Buenos Aires to try to broker a deal, and various compromises took shape. It was only because General Leopoldo Galtieri, head of the ruling military Junta, idiotically refused any of them that fighting finally broke out. Meanwhile, with one or two exceptions, the media responded to the Ministry of Defence's invitations to send reporters with the task force by assigning relatively inexperienced staff, whom they expected to have a holiday at sea for a few weeks with little to do except interview the military on board before returning to the UK. Most newspapers had already despatched correspondents to Argentina, and I was one of them. As Defence Correspondent of The Observer I was to write about the Argentine military occupation of the islands – the Malvinas, as the Argentines call them –their preparations to defend them and their plans for their future. The big prize, of course, and one which would have guaranteed a prestigious journalism award, would be an

21

exclusive story from the Falklands themselves. But could I find a way of getting there?

In fact, I got nowhere near. I ended up being arrested and put on trial for espionage. My situation was made more complicated and hazardous by the fact that when they examined my notebooks the Argentine Naval Intelligence officers, into whose hands I had fallen, found them full of details about secret military installations in the United States, and this convinced them that they had landed a big fish, some kind of super-spy. It happened this way.

One of my duties was to write about the Cold War, which was then at its height as President Reagan poured huge resources into new nuclear weapons, and the Soviet Union tried to match it. By coincidence, just before Argentina invaded the Falklands I travelled to Colorado Springs with the British Defence Secretary, John Knott, plus a retinue of Defence Ministry officials and a small group of Defence Correspondents on an RAF VC10. We were on our way to a meeting of NATO's Nuclear Planning Group, which decided matters relating to nuclear weapons within NATO. At that time the main issue was the controversial decision by the US to position cruise missiles capable of reaching the Soviet Union on the territory of those of its European allies which would accept them. Britain was one such. As we flew across the Atlantic it became evident that something unusual was going on. There was a much to-ing and fro-ing between the front cabin where Nott and the MoD officials were sitting and the cockpit, which was the communications centre with the UK. Among those on board, and in charge of the press, was Ian McDonald, the MoD's official spokesman, who was soon to appear on television every night to announce the latest news about the Falklands War in a low monotone that won him the description of the "speak your weight machine". Ian was not a typical MoD official. He was known to go to his London club at lunch time and read The Guardian, not the MoD's favourite newspaper because of its liberal views, especially on nuclear weapons. He also had an unusual sense of humour, which I appreciated, although not everyone else did. One of his personal rules was to avoid at all costs using the phrase, "no comment", as some sort of private intellectual exercise. Instead, he would prefer to respond to a journalist's question with a literary reference, such as "Shakespeare, Richard III, Act 1 Scene 3, First Murderer." For someone in my position, working for a Sunday newspaper, with time to spare it was just a bit of fun. But for the agency or daily newspaper reporters on a deadline it was infuriating. They had to scuttle off to a library to find the relevant quotation ("Talkers are not good doers"), and deduce from it whether Ian was confirming or denying the story, or just not commenting on it. "Ask about Georgia," Ian whispered to us as Nott was about to appear at the back of the plane, where we were seated, to brief us on the forthcoming NPG meeting. "Georgia?" we wondered to each other. Did he mean Georgia, the US state? Or the Soviet Republic. What was actually going on was that a group of scrap metal merchants had landed on South Georgia, a remote and inhospitable island 600 miles east of the Falkland Islands, which Argentina claimed, and were said to have raised the Argentine flag. It was not clear what they were up to, and the flag incident was later denied and may not have been true. The intruders may have been just what they said they were, a group of scrap metal merchants interested in rescuing anything of value from an old whaling station. But the Argentine military Junta, deeply unpopular at home, had already begun making bellicose noises about Argentina's "right" to the "Malvinas". The Junta turned up its collective military nose at warnings from the Argentine Foreign Ministry and from Argentina's ambassadors abroad, and totally misconstrued a British decision to withdraw the British Antarctic research ship, Endurance, on cost-cutting grounds as a signal that Britain would not lift a finger to defend these remote wild and windswept islands. After all, these were the days long before it was appreciated that the waters surrounding the islands were rich in fish and oil. The landing on South Georgia turned out to be the precursor of a full-scale invasion of the Falkland Islands, which took place during the night of April 1 and 2. The British defence force consisted of only 81 Royal Marines, and faced

23

with an invasion by 3,000 Argentines they had no choice but to surrender. But the Falklands were so far out of sight and out of mind in the South Atlantic that the British Government had categorised their population, a mere 1,820, as second-class citizens, who like the 3.5 million Chinese in Hong Kong, were British passport-holders with no automatic right of abode in Britain. Only vaguely aware of the existence of the Falklands, and completely nonplussed, I couldn't bring myself to ask Nott to "tell us about Georgia?" Pathetically, none of us asked, perhaps dismissing it as one of Ian's pranks on us.

I arrived in Colorado Springs and duly filed my story about the NPG. During my stay I was invited along with other correspondents to visit the nearby North American Aerospace Defense Command (NORAD) headquarters, deep underground in a nuclear-bomb proof bunker inside a mountain called Cheyenne. It was from here that the US monitored intercontinental ballistic missiles sites in the Soviet Union. It was linked to a line of radar stations across northern Canada, known as the DEW Line, which would provide the notorious four-minute warning of an attack if the Soviet Union were to fire its missiles over the North Pole at the United States. It was a fascinating Dr. Strangelove type of place. Some areas were labelled "no lone zones", which meant that any individual found there alone would be shot. We were informed that the security patrols within the complex were under orders to grant no exceptions. So I had the delicious privilege of terminating a phone call to the foreign desk of The Observer from a phone inside NORAD by telling them that I had to go as my group was moving on and I would myself be terminated unless I moved with them. I took copious notes as the visit was a Defence Correspondent's dream. I wrote down such information as the strength of the bunker to resist nuclear attacks in Pounds Per Square Inch – P.S.I. – initials that were later to get me into difficulty in Argentina. When the NPG meeting had finished I went to watch plutonium triggers for nuclear weapons being manufactured, mostly by poor Latin American women workers, at the Rocky Flats factory, which was nearby. I then moved on to San Francisco to visit the Ames Research Centre, where the US forces build experimental planes. After that my plan was to return home with enough material for several news stories and features.

It was now clear that the Falklands crisis had escalated, and it was decided I should fly from San Francisco to Buenos Aires. I arrived in a city that was euphoric. It was as though Argentina had just won the World Cup. There were huge demonstrations of solidarity with the Government in the streets where only a week before hostile trade unionists had been on the march. Government-sponsored advertisements on television repeated the slogan: "The recovery of our islands. Unification was very easy." Long queues of people waited to sign up to move to the Falklands, and there were plans for a press flight, with British journalists being promised priority so that they could witness for themselves the benevolence of the new rulers of the islands. I put my name down. But back home things were stirring. A naval task force was being assembled in great haste, and it began to dawn on the Argentines that the unification of which they boasted might not be very easy after all. As the task force began its 8,000-mile journey south the prospect of an Argentine Government press plane to the Falklands receded. Then on my first Saturday evening in Buenos Aires, having filed my story of the week, I found myself at a reception inside the Casa Rosada, the presidential palace, and my thoughts turned to the prospects of a unilateral initiative. I sought out Galtieri's press secretary, Colonel Osvaldo Rubio, and asked him where I was free to go in Argentina with the press card the Government had issued to me. "Go wherever you wish," he replied expansively, opening his arms wide to indicate that the whole of that vast country was open to me. I mentioned this to Simon Winchester, a reporter from the Sunday Times. Sunday newspaper journalists sometimes work together in hazardous circumstances as they have a few clear days before they need to file their stories. Simon and I had got to know each other in Lebanon during the civil war. After we had finished our week's work we would drive north from Beirut for Sunday lunch at the very agreeable harbour-side Fishing Club in Byblos, with its walls covered with photographs of film stars who had dined there in happier days. Tony Prime, an Observer photographer, had arrived in Argentina from El Salvador, where he had been covering the war there, and the three of us agreed that we would set off for the south of Argentina the next morning, which was a Sunday. We would devote a few days to trying to reach the Falklands from one of the Argentine bases that were closer to the islands, and if we failed we would return to Buenos Aires in time to find something else to write about. Nigel Hawkes, The Observer's Foreign Editor, independently made a similar suggestion when I spoke to him on the phone. The next morning when I rang Simon at his hotel he was still in bed, but agreed to get ready, and eventually the three of us arrived at Aeroparque, the Buenos Aires domestic airport, intending to travel to Comodoro Rivadavia 1,200 miles to the south. But we had no tickets, and the flight was full. In the end we went stand-by, and managed to get on the plane. If we really had been setting off on an espionage mission, as the Argentine Government was to allege, our forward planning was not very impressive. In Comodoro Rivadavia, we met the mayor and some local journalists. The mayor said that volunteers were coming forward for fire and hospital work, and also to go to the Malvinas. We went out for dinner with the local journalists at a sea front restaurant, then returned to the Austral Hotel, where we were staying, and sat late into the night talking and drinking Argentine "Old Smuggler" whisky with them. We ended with a toast to "La Paz".

The next morning we were just in time to catch a flight to Ushuaia, which we were keen to visit because it had a naval air base from where the Argentine Air Force might be flying to the Falklands. It was also an opportunity too good to miss to see Tierra Del Fuego, a wild and rugged archipelago, much of it unexplored, that stretched out towards the South Pole at the tip of South America. A copy of the South American Handbook which we carried with us stated that Ushuaia, the capital of the eastern (Argentine) half of the territory, was: " the most southerly town in the world; its steep streets overlook the green waters of the Beagle Channel, named after the ship in which Charles Darwin sailed the Channel in 1832. It is reached from Buenos Aires by ship (monthly, 9 days) or plane (5 hours)." We flew first to Rio Gallegos in southern Patagonia, where we changed flights, and it was here that I got the first whiff of possible trouble ahead. We were now close to the Falklands, and there was a lot of military activity. Argentine Air Force Mirages and Skyhawks flying from Rio Gallegos were clearly visible because the airport runway was used by both civilian and military aircraft. Tony began taking photographs of them, as photographers are wont to do, and an official asked him to stop. He then disappeared, only to reappear a few minutes later saying that he had been into the lavatory, climbed onto the seat and tried to take photos through the window. But he had been thwarted because of dirt on the outside, which he had been unable to remove. Meanwhile, Simon was looking through his binoculars and identifying the planes in a loud voice.

We then flew on to the next Argentine air base, which was at Rio Grande in Tierra Del Fuego. This time we were in a Fokker Friendship, a propeller-driven plane belonging to LADE (Lineas Areas Del Estado), an airline owned by the Argentine Air Force. It had large windows, and flew low, weaving along valleys in between snow-capped mountains, with glimpses of the sea. Tony began photographing again. A steward told him to stop. So he went to sit in a window seat at the back of the near-empty plane, and it was with a sinking feeling that I could hear the "click click" of his camera. On the ground at Rio Grande a woman in a fur coat came to us with an official, and said she had seen us taking photographs. We were taken to a room and questioned, but released. "Bitch!" Simon shouted at the woman. Despite this confrontation, we then had an amiable chat with the local manager of Aerolineas Argentinas as we waited for our flight to Ushuaia. He told that us he had been to the Malvinas, that they were beautiful, but there was nothing much there. Outside next to the runway around 200 Argentine troops in green uniforms

Ushuaia in the Antarctic winter

descended from an Argentine Air Force C-130 transport plane and sat on the grass, with no attempt being made to hide their movements. Later Tony told me that as he had done his national service in the RAF he had taken photographs of beaches from the plane "in case they were useful to our forces", in other words as possible landing sites by Royal Marines. I am glad that I did not know that until much later, or I would have been furious.

We caught the flight to Ushuaia, from where we would make our final attempt to reach the Falklands. Among the passengers were a soldier with a machine gun and another with a revolver – a sign that these were not normal times. As we walked down the steps of the plane at Ushuaia a photographer took photographs of us, and it was now clear that our movements were being monitored. But I thought little of it, expecting perhaps that we would be ordered to return to Buenos Aires. We checked into the Canal Beagle Hotel, from where we enjoyed a superb view of the Beagle Channel and the snow-covered mountains of Navarin and Hoste Islands across the water. Our Spanish was inadequate, and in the hotel register, under "Estado", which I thought meant "civilian" or "military" I wrote "civilian". In fact, I should have written my occupation. The error was later taken as evidence that I was not really a journalist. That evening we went for a stroll around Ushuaia, a town of around 7,000, consisting of wooden buildings painted in pastel shades, and then to a local restaurant called Tante Elvira – it's still there. We dined on centollas (local bright red crabs) followed by fresh local fish dishes, and drank four bottles of Argentine rosé wine. It was to be our last meal in freedom for three months.

The next morning, having failed in our attempts to reach the Falklands we set off back to Buenos Aires, and caught an early LADE flight to Rio Grande, where we could transfer onto an Aereolinas Argentinas jet. As we boarded the plane at Ushuaia a photographer took photos of us again. At Rio Grande we were sitting in the terminal next to the gate from which we were to depart when we were approached by a naval officer accompanied by two sailors pointing guns at us. "Excuse me," the officer said, "Will you please come with me in a bus." I remember saying: "We're not going with you. We're on our way back to Buenos Aires." The two sailors then poked their guns at us menacingly, and I saw the strength of the officer's argument. As we picked up our bags to accompany him he uttered the immortal words: "For you the war is over."

Argentinian gunboat in Beagle Channel

Ushuaia and Mount Olivia at dawn

CHAPTER THREE

TUG OF WAR

A s they took us away Simon managed to hand a card to a passenger with the contact details of Kenneth Clark, a reporter with the Daily Telegraph, who was at the Sheraton Hotel in Buenos Aires, in the hope that he would tell him what had happened to us. We were taken into a small office at the airport, where they opened our bags, and began to list every item. I was told that we had been arrested by the Navy, but that the Navy did not trust the local police. So, a local civilian had "volunteered" to witness the opening of our bags and sign off the list of our possessions. It turned out to be a bigger job than they had bargained for, even though we were carrying only overnight bags. I was a frequent traveller, and had a collection of free toiletries from five star hotels. To my immense embarrassment I had no less than 25 small bars of soap in my bag, every one of which had to be individually listed. Eventually, the job was done, and the civilian appended his signature as evidence that all our property had been accounted for. The naval officer said that they were doing this because they did not trust the police. He said we would be handed over to the care of the Swiss embassy, which was responsible for British interests since the British embassy had packed its bags and gone across the River Plate to Uruguay. In fact, we were led out of the airport and put in an ambulance that doubled up as a police van. The three of us sat in the back on an old tyre with a policeman sitting among us, and were driven into town. When I tried to speak one of the police prodded me in the chest, put a finger to his lips and said: "Shh!"

We were taken to the local police station, and put into separate cells. Mine measured ten paces by eight. I calculated that it was about 3pm. It was a sunny afternoon, and there was a small high window, through which the sun cast a shadow. I decided to pace around the cell doing figures of eight, counting the seconds and putting marks on the wall with my fingernail at regular intervals to show the progress of the sun's shadow. By this means, I reckoned, I could work out the time and maintain some contact with reality. I remembered having read a book by a Reuters correspondent who had been held prisoner in Beijing, and had used a similar walking arrangement to keep account of the time and the days. My spirits were high. I was now guaranteed to have my story published in the paper. That had been my preoccupation since we had failed to reach the Falklands. Our trip to the south had now been worthwhile. I assumed that it was only a matter of time before we were put on a plane to Buenos Aires. A number of my colleagues had been briefly imprisoned in other countries, and then emerged to write about "My Night in an African Hell Hole" or something like that. Not only did I have a publishable story for the following weekend, but I had now joined a particular élite, that of journalists who had been thrown into jail for just doing their job. I had little doubt that I would be back in Buenos Aires before the weekend in time to file my story about my brief encounter with the Argentine prison system. It never occurred to me that the Argentines would invoke the full panoply of their espionage laws against us for our over-enthusiastic reporting. What I failed to realise was that although I had reported on many wars in the past my own country had not been involved.

The next morning we were driven to the military side of the airport, where an Argentine Air Force Electra long-range reconnaissance plane was waiting. I asked an Air force officer what was going to happen to us, and he replied: "Nothing". But I was starting to become sceptical about their answers. In fact, we were flown all the way back to Buenos Aires. The flight took seven or eight hours, and there were several stops on the way. During the flight we were not allowed to talk to each other, and during one stop we were ordered to stare at a spot in front of us and not look out of the window while we were on the ground. I believe that the reason was that we were at the Comandante Espora Naval air base, home of Argentina's Third Squadron, equipped with Skyhawks, which would soon be in action against the British fleet. I was now desperately hungry, and drooled as trays of food were carried past us to the cabin crew. But we were given nothing to eat. We landed in Buenos Aires, and were taken to a naval air station close to the main Estezia Airport. There at last we were given a meal, which included steak, in what appeared to be an officers' mess. While we were eating, an Argentine official who was carrying our documents in three large envelopes spoke on the phone. At one point there was a phrase which I could understand: "the custody is totally naval". We spent the night and the next day in the guards' bedroom, which was filled with bunk beds which stayed empty. And the next night too. The building was close to the end of the civilian runway, and through the window I watched civilian flights – Air France, Iberia, even British Airways - taxi to a point close enough for me to see the passengers through their windows, turn and take off for Europe. We could also see every vehicle that entered the prison compound, and as each one arrived and the barrier was raised our hopes rose too that after a short interval the cell door would be unlocked, we would be taken outside, driven over to the airport and put on a plane. Later I was to discover that a tug-of-war was going on. We were a prize catch. The Government in Buenos Aires wanted to keep us, but the Navy, which controlled the whole of southern Argentina, including the judicial system, insisted that we were theirs, and that we should be taken back south. At one point I tried to force the issue. I wrote on a page from my notebook: "May we please speak to a senior officer." I knocked on the cell door. It was opened by a nervous young Argentine soldier who pointed his gun at me. I gave him a big smile, slowly raised one arm into the air, let the paper flutter to the floor, turned my back on him and went back inside the room. The result: nothing. The next morning we were off on our travels again, this time to my dismay, all the way back to the south of Argentina. Once again an Argentine Air Force Electra flew us there. Two Argentine Ministry of Defence officials accompanied us. We got chatting, and I wrote a note to Margaret (my wife), handed it to one of the officials with some money and asked him to post it, to let her know I was alright. It never reached my home.

At Rio Grande we were taken to the local police station, and then to the office of the police station chief, who addressed us in Spanish. One word I distinctly remember was "lamentablemente", from which, I immediately worked out that the news was not good for us. In fact, we were to be flown back to Ushuaia. They put us in a large cell with double bunk beds. The mattresses were filthy, but there were coarse clean sheets on top of them, and I slept well, even though the lights were left on all night. At 6 am we were taken back to the airport and flown south, again in an Electra, accompanied by the same two security men. It was a turbulent flight, and the propeller-driven plane, bumped along. In gaps between the clouds I glimpsed snow-covered mountains and deep valleys through the large picture windows. This time there was no question of taking notes or photographs. To my surprise there were two journalists on the plane. They were from the Argentine news magazine, Siete Dias, and we agreed to talk to them and be photographed. I asked them to inform our newspapers about what had happened to us, and wrote a note to that effect. I saw the result later in the week, and noted that I was unflatteringly described as having "a ginger beard and small nervous eyes", and that Simon "gave the impression of being the most important and most intellectual of the three". They published my note in their article, but did not pass it on. Thanks, colleagues! But I salute their enterprise in getting on the plane. We landed in Ushuaia and were led down the steps of the plane. In any other circumstances I would have marvelled at the spectacular amphitheatre of mountains and been grateful for the privilege of seeing it. Not this time. Next to the runway a line of black official cars manned by officials in black suits were waiting, as though expecting coffins for a funeral. Heading this impressive reception committee was Comisario José Barrozo, head of the prison at Ushuaia, a short dapper man in his mid-forties with a neat moustache, whom we were to come to know well. We were put into separate cars, driven two miles to the local prison in the centre of the town and placed in separate cells. The first thing that happened there was that I was made to strip, lie naked on a prison cot and be photographed. A small man in a white coat arrived. It was a chilling moment as I caught sight of some kind of electrical equipment on a trolley in the corridor. Was the man in the white coat, who now began to examine me, checking my ability to withstand torture? Were we to join the "desaparecidos", the thousands who had disappeared during Argentina's Dirty War, many of them at the hands of the Navy, in whose hands we now were? Yet he seemed pleasant enough. He asked me in English what day it was and what my name was. I got the day wrong, but he didn't seem to notice. He shook my hand, said: "Good luck", and left. Later I was told that he was a police doctor, and had merely been ensuring that I had not been harmed by the Navy. The equipment had been for welding a cell door that had broken.

Ushuaia Prison

'THE END OF THE WORLD'

CHAPTER FOUR

THE MOST SOUTHERLY JAIL IN THE WORLD

Ushuaia was a naval base, where the headquarters of the
Argentine Naval Southern Area Command was located, and
there was also a naval air base next to the airport. I knew
something about the place because from time to time it had been in
the news as a result of a long-running dispute with Chile over the
border in Tierra Del Fuego and the Beagle Channel. Argentine fast
torpedo boats were based there, and both governments had risked
a serious accident as Argentine and Chilean gun boats indulged in
games of "chicken" in the disputed waters by racing towards each
other and trying to force the other to give way. I had even travelled
along the Beagle Channel in an Argentine Navy supply ship a few
years earlier to visit three disputed islands in the Beagle Channel for
a story for The Observer. I thought it prudent not to mention this
fact to the Argentines. In the past Ushuaia's prison had been the
main reason for the town's existence. It had been what Devil's Island
had been to France or Tasmania to Britain, a remote island from
which there was almost no possibility of escape on which to house
the country's most dangerous offenders. While the prison continued
to be Ushuaia's raison d'être the Argentine Government built up the
local population in order to reinforce its sovereignty over Tierra Del
Fuego. The original prison no longer existed as a prison. It had been
closed 35 years earlier, although the old building still stood within
the perimeter of the naval headquarters compound and was later to
become a museum. The prison to which I was taken was the local
town jail and was in the local police station. It was smaller than the

original prison, and consisted of a single row of cells along one side of a corridor. The corridor was about 25 paces long, and on the other side of it were a dining room and a leisure room with a black and white TV and a table tennis table. But the cells and their hard metal frame beds were almost identical to the cells in the old prison. The three of us were now in a single cell that had a double metal bunk at one side, and a single bed at the other, which we had to stand on its end against a wall so that we could move around the cell. The facilities were poor. At the end there was a bathroom with a row of three urinals, where prisoners squatted over an open hole in the concrete floor, and a shower with cold water. Experience in Iran with similar "Islamic" lavatories came in useful now. At the entrance to the prison corridor were two sets of metal gates with heavy locks and chains, and in the space between them was another cell that was used for people who were accommodated for the night for various reasons. As it was a local jail, most but not all the prisoners were inside for minor offences. We were a sensation. On our arrival the entire prison was "locked down". All the other prisoners were confined to their cells, and total silence was imposed. I sat there in the eerie silence until the evening when there was a rattling of lock and chain, a key turned, the door opened and a prison guard indicated with an arm that I and my colleagues could walk up and down the corridor. It was exercise time. As we paced up and down we heard a noise. A cell door opened and shut again almost immediately, and three apples came rolling towards us along the ground. It was the first sign that while we may have been dangerous international spies in the eyes of the Argentine authorities, as far as the other prisoners were concerned we were in a similar situation to them. This was to be very important. It was also reassuring that the figure I glimpsed before he disappeared behind his cell door appeared to be wearing jeans and a tee-shirt, and not a suit with arrows, or even worse the ghastly yellow and black striped uniforms that made them look like wasps, which the prisoners had had to wear in the old Ushuaia prison. Later I was to discover that our benefactor was Humbert, a Chilean businessman

Headquarters of the Argentine Navy's Southern Area Command, Ushuaia

who was in prison for stealing whisky.

Late that evening the key turned in the lock again and the cell door opened to reveal a tall stiff-backed man with sleek swept-back hair, and penetrating blue eyes. He wore the dark-blue uniform of an Argentine Marine officer, heavy with gold braid. He introduced himself as Capitan de Fragata (Commander) Juan Carlos Grieco. He said he was responsible for our welfare, and asked if we suffered "anxiety". "Yes", we said. "Is it supportable?" he asked. We were to come to know him well. In fact, he was much more than a welfare officer. He was the senior military officer involved in the case against us, and the right-hand man of Rear Admiral Horacio Zaratiegui, naval commander of the Southern Area, whose fiefdom extended to the Falklands. Zaratiegui's headquarters was just down the road from the prison, and from there the admiral took an intense interest in us. He considered us to be his prize catch. Grieco got to know a lot about me and my colleagues. A fairly fluent English speaker, he received transcripts of all phone calls, and perused letters sent to us and by us. Grieco doubled up as official head of the Tierra Del Fuego Territorial Police. So he was superior to Barrozo who was a professional detective. As a naval officer he had no previous experience of the prison service. Not only was Argentina a military dictatorship, but the extreme South was the Navy's bailiwick.

On Sunday afternoon the judge appeared in the prison. A middle-aged man in gold-rimmed spectacles, he introduced himself as Carlos Sagastume. He said he was a retired naval officer, but now a civilian judge. He insisted that the judiciary were independent of the military. "Have faith in Argentine justice," he told us. "Remove from your minds any thoughts of 'Midnight Express'". Each of us would be given an official prison number and our case would also have an official number. At the time I had no idea how important this bureaucratic procedure was. Starting the next morning, the judge said, he would be asking us lots of questions. For now, we would be in the same cell to keep each other company, but after that we would be separated until the questioning had ended. He then left. There followed a farcical moment when there was a knock on our cell door. It was the prison staff who realised after locking us in that they had left the key on the inside of the door, so couldn't get in. We handed the key back to them.

By now we had been missing for nearly a week, and there was no indication that there was concern in London. When I had failed to file a story the previous Saturday The Observer had not been worried. However, The Sunday Times had recently had a reporter taken prisoner in Somalia and had delayed raising the alarm, with the result that his captors had refused to believe that he was a journalist, putting his life in grave danger. Chastened by this experience the Sunday Times insisted on alerting the Foreign Office, which issued a statement. The BBC reported the announcement, and The Times carried a story on its front page saying that three British journalists were missing. The Argentine Government then admitted that it was holding us. We knew about this because we had been allowed to keep a short wave radio which could pick up the BBC World Service

Concern over British journalists

Concern is growing over three British journalists in Argentina who have not been heard from since Sunday. Mr Simon Winchester of *The Sunday Times*, and Mr Ian Mather and Mr Tony Prime, of *The Observer*, left Buenos Aires for a tour of Argentine ports.

The Times, 17 April 1982

programmes beamed to Latin America. In my diary I wrote: "Friday 16 April. The BBC reported there was concern about the whereabouts of three British journalists. A few World Service bulletins later we heard that the Editor of The Observer had issued a statement saying that everything possible would be done to secure our release."

At least we were now back on the radar screen, and soon our imprisonment was made official. I was taken into an outer office where two men were sitting at a desk. One typed out a document, which stated that I had been arrested at the time I had been brought back to Ushuaia, that my prison number was 544 and that our case number was 8339. Later I discovered that I should have been highly relieved. This was a key moment. Until then any of the three of us could have disappeared without trace. From now on that was not possible because we were official prisoners. Unaware of the significance of the document I was depressed. The three of us had just agreed that it would be better if we did not discuss with each other what we had seen or done prior to our arrest so as not to appear as a "team". So later I was mortified to discover that during his interrogation Tony Prime had described me as the leader of our "mission", and claimed that he had taken photographs on orders from me. The result was that the bail money for me was the highest of the three because, according to the court documents, I had special

41

connections with "the British War Ministry". I did not discover this until ten years later. Equally galling was a remark by Tony that as a former member of the Royal Air Force during his national service he had decided to take aerial photographs of beaches in Tierra Del Fuego from the plane "in case they were of use to the British forces." By that he meant potential landing sites for the Royal Marines. These photographs were to prove impossible to explain.

The three of us were crammed into one small cell, and during the night a prison officer repeatedly switched on the cell light from the outside and peered at us through the "Judas Hole". It was difficult to get any sleep. To try to maintain a sense of perspective I decided early on to keep a diary if I could get my hands on some writing paper. Somehow I managed to acquire various bits of paper and envelopes, and started writing brief notes. Later, after the Swiss had taken over the consular role of the British after the British embassy closed in Buenos Aires, a Swiss diplomat managed to visit us. He went into the town and bought me a spiral-bound exercise book with an incongruous montage of skin diving equipment, goggles and flippers on the cover, and I transferred my notes to it. On the fly leaf I wrote a prison motto I had dreamed up for myself: Pacienca. Tranquilidad. Valor. Humor. Patience. Calm. Courage. Humour. I wrote the same words on a piece of paper, which I hung over a rail at the bottom of my bed, so that it was the first thing I looked at each morning.

A point about the diary. Whenever you read a prison diary, especially one written by someone whose life is in danger, don't expect a totally honest account. I can vouch for the fact that the desire for personal survival is so overwhelming every word that you write is influenced by how it will be perceived by the jailers. Even the most personal diary is written with the knowledge that one's captors could seize it and read it any time. The events described in my diary are all true, but my portrayal of every agent of the Argentine state whom I encountered, as being entirely benevolent was done with half an eye on trying to keep them well-disposed towards me. They were not at all brutal, and I bear them no ill. But I was fully aware that every word I wrote could have been used against me had they so wished. The fact that no one ever confiscated my diary, even at times of great tension in the Falklands War, is greatly to their credit.

Our interrogation was due to begin on Monday morning. But this being South America nothing had happened by lunch time. All morning we tramped up and down the corridor staring at the ground. Then we were told that the judge worked from 2 pm until 8pm. Eventually Grieco appeared, and told us that the Public Prosecutor, who was normally referred to as "The Fiscal" (district attorney), was presenting evidence against us first. "The prosecution have much evidence against you. It means your situation is not good," he said ominously. Tony was called first, around 6pm. From time to time I tapped three times on the wall of the adjoining cell, where I expected him to be, and eventually heard three taps back. Then I heard his voice, which sounded as though it was coming through a tunnel. He had found an old piece of flexible pipe under his bed, twisted it into a horse-shoe and poked it through the bars of his window and into my cell. I put my ear to it. He was not able to say much, except that the interrogation would continue at 10 am the next day, and that "Isabel says there is good hope". I had heard that Isabel Hilton of the Sunday Times, a fluent Spanish speaker, had managed to beaver her way into the judge's office to act as an extra interpreter. I had still to meet her.

Then it was my turn to be questioned. In my diary I wrote: "Tuesday, 20 April. I was taken to court just before 11 am in a car with three burly men. They drove very slowly so that Argentine TV could first film me leaving the prison, then pack their cameras and film me arriving at the court-house. One of the guards wiped the window so I could be filmed inside the car." In normal times Ushuaia was a quiet backwater. Now with the arrest of three British "spies", it found itself in the news spotlight, and journalists from far and wide had descended on the town. I managed a wintry smile as I recognised colleagues among the crowd of reporters standing in the snow outside the court. Philip Hayden, the BBC reporter, pulled the old trick of shouting "Ian" as I got out of the car, so that I would instinctively look round and my face would be on TV. That evening when I watched the local TV I was the first item on the local news, and it seemed that my arrest and court appearance were the biggest event since Charles Darwin sailed up the Beagle Channel. I watched the footage of myself being bundled in and out of the car on my way to and from the prison. Every time there was the same chilling subtitle on the screen: "British spy".

Outside the judge's office was a brass plaque that indicated that his jurisdiction encompassed the "Malvinas", South Georgia and Argentine Antarctica, as well as Tierra Del Fuego. Later when we were having a conversation with him he told us that he had always been proud of the fact that the Malvinas were under his jurisdiction, though he had never been able to go there. He then produced half a dozen photographs. They were of the control tower and the airport terminal at Port Stanley, the Falklands capital, and had clearly been taken in a hurry as they were out of focus and at a crazy angle. He had risked travelling to the Falklands in an Argentine Air Force C130, spent a few minutes on the ground to take photos, and then flown back to Argentina. "I went because I wanted to know the islands. See them. Touch them. It was an incredible emotion," he said. He was also proud of the fact that Argentine Antarctica was part of his domain. Once when I happened to refer to Ushuaia as the most southerly city in the world, he said: "Esperanza". An interpreter explained that Esperanza in Argentine Antarctica made this claim. I said that I didn't think it should qualify as it was only a scientific and meteorological station. The judge disagreed, and I was in no position to argue.

The Argentine system is "inquisitorial", based largely on the West European model. There is no trial by jury, and the judge plays an active role. An accused person is questioned by the judge, and the prosecution and defence lawyers then make their submissions. When the preliminary questioning is over the judge decides whether there is a case to answer. If he decides that there is then it is up to the two sets of lawyers to build their cases, a process that can take weeks

The author (right) being escorted to court

or months. The interrogation took place in the judge's office. The judge sat at a glass-topped desk and the other people in the room sat in a semi-circle in front of him. Behind him were rows of legal books and on the wall facing him was an ivory crucifix with Christ in agony. Those in the room were his assistant, Raoul Richieri, the Federal District Prosecutor, or "Fiscal", Santiago Kiernan, who was wearing a greenish Harris tweed jacket that could have been made in the Hebrides, and our defence lawyer, Guillermo (Willy) Balaban, who had been hired by the two newspapers and whom I had never met. Willy introduced himself to me, and said he had been up at 4 am to fly from Buenos Aires. There were also an official interpreter, Marghuerita Vasquez, a typist, whose name I did not discover and a tall blonde woman who was also acting as interpreter. She must have thought me a bit odd when I explained some of the facts about British journalism to her. For it took some time before I realised that she was in fact Isabel Hilton, a Spanish-speaking reporter from the Sunday Times, who had persuaded the judge that she could play a useful role. The three of us much appreciated her presence, and in any case hers was a considerable journalistic coup. Much of the questioning was based on my notebooks, and there was particular interest in the fact that I had been inside a top secret US establishment, The "Fiscal" genuinely believed he was in the presence of an international spy of considerable status. He asked me to explain the meaning of the phrase: "P.S.I. is classified". I explained that "Pounds per Square Inch" was a measurement of strength to withstand a nuclear attack, and I told him what the strength was for that particular bunker. He also asked about references to various screens I had seen showing details of US and Soviet missiles. Then came what he thought was his coup de grace. "What means did you use to gain entry to this top secret US base?" He really thought that I must have either climbed in, or disguised myself as a member of the Strategic Air Command staff and slipped past the security at the gate. "I was invited by the American Government, as one of a group of British reporters", I replied. The Fiscal's face was a picture of dismay as he saw his future as the Johnnie Cochran of the Argentine legal system crumble. The judge looked up to the ceiling, and repeated robotically: "He was invited inside by the US Government!" It began to dawn on the judge that I might be a genuine reporter after all. I might be using this role as a cover for espionage. Nevertheless, I was definitely a reporter. The judge then gave short shrift to other ludicrous pieces of so-called evidence, which had been listed as espionage material. A photograph had appeared in a local newspaper showing my short wave radio with the antenna extended, indicating that it was for sending and receiving messages, and a booklet with the title, "Key". The short wave radio was simply that, nothing more, and was capable of neither receiving nor transmitting messages. The booklet entitled "Key" was from my hotel room in San Francisco, and was simply a free guide to what to do and what was on in the city. Neither of these items was ever mentioned again. Even the fact that I had "researcher" in my passport as my profession did not seem to concern the judge too much. I had been concerned when I discovered that the word had been translated into Spanish as "investigator", which I thought was a little to close for comfort to "spy". I was also amused when the prosecution revealed that Tony was a "representative", and Simon a

So-called espionage materials

"commercial consultant". But I need not have worried on this score. The judge took the intelligent view that if a spy wanted to disguise himself as a journalist, he would make sure that he had journalist as his profession in his passport, whereas a genuine journalist might not for the reasons I explained in Chapter 1.

I was then questioned about a list of the names of the officers of a British submarine which was found in a notebook. This was a very unfortunate coincidence. The submarine was the Onyx, on which I had spent a night at sea in the English Channel to write an article for The Observer colour magazine. I explained that I had promised to send the crew copies of the article, that it had only recently been published as the magazine section had very long deadlines, and that I had not had time to send the copies. I added that the court officials could find the article easily enough if they wished to, and that in any case I certainly would not have been carrying a piece of paper with a list of British submarine officers if I were a spy? I was also questioned about Kenneth Clarke. I explained that he was a Daily

Telegraph reporter, whom I had known for years, since we had both worked in Manchester on rival newspapers. It emerged that Simon's attempt to get a message to Kenneth Clarke about our arrest was being misinterpreted. Simon's had been a perfectly natural reaction in a country where so many people had disappeared. But the Argentine Navy evidently thought that we were part of a wide conspiracy, and had made a ham-fisted attempt to warn our fellow-conspirators. Even a trip I had made to the airport lavatory just before our arrest was interpreted as a desperate attempt to get rid of a transmitter. I was told that the lavatory had been searched and nothing found. Ugh! Yet they failed to take the logical step of arresting Ken Clarke. They had all the details about him because he was accredited to the Argentine Government as a journalist in exactly the same way as we were, and he was sitting in the Sheraton Hotel in Buenos Aires along with all the other foreign journalists. His by-line from Buenos Aires was in the Daily Telegraph or Sunday Telegraph every day. Yet no one in authority even approached him. The fact was the Argentine Government were too cowardly to raid the Sheraton Hotel, where the international press were staying, because of the worldwide furore their action would have created. So Ken Clarke and his alleged role were deliberately left as loose ends by the prosecution in Ushuaia.

In going through my notebooks the judge was eager to move quickly through my earlier reporting from Buenos Aires which related to such things as the diplomatic mission of Alexander Haig, the US Secretary of State, a large demonstration in Mayo Square, interviews with volunteers for the Falklands and a visit to the Hurlingham Club to interview polo-playing Anglo-Argentines. I cannot resist recalling that the secretary of the latter, who rejoiced in the splendid name of Shakespeare Miles, made me welcome but ordered the photographer to remain outside as his profession was not socially acceptable at the club! The judge was interested only in the air and naval bases starting with Comodoro Rivadavia. It quickly became apparent that many of the notes in my notebook could be interpreted in either of two ways. They were either the natural jottings of a reporter in a war zone

```
Such data are of interest to foreign powers which could be in conflict
with our country.  It is affirmed that in view of the special
circumstances prevailing in Argentina, and due to the fact that the
accused are specifically English citizens, the possibility of their
having been engaged in simple journalistic activities is discarded.
END OF TAPE 4
```

Extract from Argentine Intelligence report

who was gathering material for a newspaper, or they were eye-witness information of a military nature intended to be useful to an enemy. Of course, they were the former, but the Argentines decided that they were the latter. The Head of Intelligence at Ushuaia Naval Base, Naval Lieutenant Horacio Vargas, and his staff, had the unenviable task of deciphering my four notebooks, which covered my time in the US and Argentina. They managed to do so. I never had the pleasure of meeting them, but theirs was a highly professional achievement since my scribble consisted of a mixture of my own abbreviations and genuine short hand symbols. But even my own brand of short hand that I had developed over the years was made to look like evidence that I was a spy. The Argentine Naval Intelligence report concluded: "All this was set down in telegraphic form with a special method of synthesis (i.e. method of abbreviating his known notes)." After listing all my notes about military aircraft, Argentine troops etc that I had seen at airports en route to Ushuaia, the intelligence officer had written: "Such data are of interest to foreign powers which could be in conflict with our country. It is affirmed that in view of the special circumstances prevailing in Argentina, and due to the fact that the accused are specifically English citizens, the possibility of their having been engaged in simple journalistic activities is discarded." The same was true of Tony's photographs. Where he had taken two photographs of the same aircraft, Argentine Naval Intelligence

Extract from Argentine Naval Intelligence accusation

concluded that there were "stereoscopic pairs" of photographs, to be used by British intelligence to construct a three-dimensional photograph.

An amusing moment occurred when I was explaining some notes I had made in the lounge at Rio Grande airport about the types of military aircraft I had seen while sitting around waiting for the connection to Buenos Aires just before we were arrested. I told the judge that we had got chatting to the pilot of the Tierra Del Fuegan regional government plane, had asked him what type of military aircraft we could see, and that he had told us. The Tierra Del Fuegan plane, a bright red Lear jet, stood on the apron outside the window, and we also asked the pilot if there was any chance of a lift over to the Falklands. What a coup that would have been to arrive in the "Malvinas" on the Tierra Del Fuegan government plane! Unsurprisingly, the answer was no. But the pilot had not seemed particularly shocked at our request. The judge took off his glass, looked around the room and said with a shake of his head: "The pilot of the government plane told them!"

Back in the prison and feeling rather smug about what I considered to have been a bravura performance I decided to write a note in Spanish and hand it to the night duty officer. Using a Spanish edition of Readers Digest to find approximate words and phrases I wrote that as the judge had promised that after interrogation we would no longer be in solitary confinement, and as Tony and I had been questioned, technically the two of us should now be allowed to share the same cell. Simon should join us after his interrogation. To my surprise, the effect was immediate. My cell door was unlocked, and so was Tony's. I had already developed a mild phobia about locked cell doors. I wrote in my diary: "When anyone appears to be about close the cell door from the outside I leap up and shout: 'Don't close the door!' I wonder if I shall be as nervous about closed doors when I get back, home." In fact, for several months afterwards I was. Then thankfully it wore off.

My contacts book remained of great concern to me. Like all journalists' contacts books it contained the names, addresses and phone numbers, including home phone numbers, of contacts I had built up over many years. Many of these were in the defence world, especially the British defence establishment. What concerned me most was that I remembered that I had written the address of the headquarters of MI6, the British intelligence service, on a corner of a page from the London Evening Standard and placed it loose somewhere in my contacts book. As the realisation grew that Argentine Naval Intelligence was interpreting everything we had written as a threat to Argentine security this piece of paper became an obsession, and I could think of little else. Simon later wrote that "as far as I am concerned it never existed". This was untrue. I decided to confide in Cal McCrystal, a Sunday Times reporter with an Irish passport who was allowed to remain in Ushuaia for some time and who gave us immense support. He promised to do something about it. On his next visit he said to me: "the problem of the M1 motorway is solved." Later Willy, our lawyer, told me what he had done. He had gone to the judge's office, where the judge was working on some papers, and had asked to borrow my contacts book to check some facts in it. He had then gone outside for a cigarette. There he had found the piece of paper, set light to it with the cigarette and burned it.

The next stage in the proceedings against us was for Judge Sagastume to give his decision on whether there was a case to answer, and for that we had to wait a day or two. The widespread view of our colleagues and of those involved in our case at the two newspapers was that it was unlikely to be more than a formality. It was obvious that we were journalists. We had perhaps over-stepped the mark, and would be deported, after having our notebooks and cameras confiscated. When at last around 6 pm on Friday 23 April we were summoned to the judge's office it was empty. Instead, a lengthy typewritten document lay on his desk. In my diary I wrote: "It was left to Isabel Hilton (of the Sunday Times) to read the verdict. Gradually, as she translated it emerged that not only were we being accused of taking illegal photos, but also of having the intention to spy for the British government and working as a team. It was all ghastly, and I held my head in my hands. I felt sorry for Isabel." We were to be held in prison pending trial for espionage, and it emerged that the prosecution was asking for prison sentences of two years and two months for Tony and myself, and for two years and six months for Simon because he had previously taken photographs in the Falkland Islands. That itself did not sound too bad. The problem was: could the Argentine justice system be trusted? At a council of war afterwards with the lawyers, Isabel and Hugh O'Shaughnessy of The Observer, the mood was black. Hugh went around muttering: 'Shit and botheration!' As well as being extremely concerned about what might now happen to us I was angry. If we really had intended to embark on a spying mission to the south we would have made some plans.. We would have ensured that our passports described us as journalists. We would have taken the trouble to book air tickets in advance. Once embarked on our mission our behaviour would have been completely different. We would not have gone around openly asking questions about Argentine military aircraft. We would have avoided drawing attention to ourselves. I was furious that our intelligence had been insulted by making us look like a bunch of bumbling amateurs. Bizarrely, as in the US justice system, we were allowed to hold a press conference, which took place in the prison officers section, and I was able to let off steam. I decided to try to hit back hard. I said that we were being victimised because we were British. I said that we had done nothing worse than a French photographer, who had been caught taking photos of Argentine Super Etendard war planes, and had then merely had his film confiscated before being sent back to Buenos

Aires. Could this be because France was supplying Argentina with Exocet missiles for use against the British, I asked sarcastically? One of the Argentine newspapers had accused us of coming south on a "fifth rate spying mission". Surely a sophisticated man like the judge didn't believe a word of that! "Are you listening? Do you hear what he's saying?" Hugh kept asking the Argentine journalists. Whether they were listening or not, I do not know. But none of my words got into print in Argentina. One aspect of the day's events stayed in my mind: Sagastume's strange behaviour. Despite being treated with great deference by the lawyers and his officials, always being referred to as "Your Honour" he had not been able to look us in the eye on this occasion. He had hidden himself away rather than face us with the "bad news". It was an interesting weakness, which was not confined to him. Others connected with the Ushuaia legal system always sought to avoid face-to-face confrontations with us, and would even back down if presented with no other option. They appeared to lack self-confidence. Perhaps living and working in such an isolated spot they were unsure how to deal with creatures like us, who must have seemed to have come from another planet. I do not know the reason. But it was definitely a weakness that might be exploited later, if the opportunity ever arose.

Ushuaia, seen from the Beagle Channel

The Beagle Channel and the Belgrano Memorial

CHAPTER FIVE

THE CRIMINALS OF TIERRA DEL FUEGO

My imprisonment now entered a new phase. It was clear that I was going to be there for the duration of the war at least, and perhaps a long time after that. I had to settle down as best I could and let the war take its course. The best hope now lay in an impressive worldwide publicity campaign on our behalf that the two newspapers had already launched. At first the three of us were allowed out of our cell only during "siesta" time when the other prisoners were locked up. But eventually we won a concession from Barrozo, the de facto prison governor, that we could mix with the other prisoners by day, but not at night. Barrozo explained that at night there was a danger from the other prisoners. He moved his hand across his throat. During the night the rattle of the chains on the gate at the end of the prison corridor would wake me up as I had no idea what if anything was about to happen. Sometimes I never found out what had been going on during the night. At other times the next morning a new inmate would be there. There was a regular unlocking and locking of the gates and tramping of boots at weekends, but this was of less concern as this was the time when drunks were brought in from a local night club. We were in a cell close to the entrance, separated from the other cells by a locked gate. The other prisoners greeted us through the gate. One pointed to himself and said "Zoo. Panthers" and then to us and said "Leones", lions. I hardly felt like a lion. Yet some of the other prisoners seemed to be afraid of us, as though we were highly trained professional spies. I wrote in my diary: "I have come to realise that not only have we nothing to fear from the other prisoners, but that they are a bit afraid of us. It may have been the articles in the magazines portraying us as James Bond types with photographs of Roger Moore that did it. Grieco used to joke about us as spies. When we were lined up together against the prison wall for a photograph he jabbed a finger at us in turn and said "0. 0. 7" . When I put up my fists in mock boxing mode one of the prisoners visibly jumped. Yet I could not box to save my life." Indeed, I must have looked a pathetic sight as I had lost weight because of the bad food, and had to walk around holding up my trousers. Later when things settled down I put on weight.

In fact, the other prisoners could hardly have been friendlier. To their minds the confrontation that mattered was not Argentina versus Britain, but the Argentine legal system against us, and that meant all of us. They spread their arms out and made aeroplane noises indicating that they believed we would soon be flying home. We were all in the same situation as we sat in our blacked-out cells and listened as the air-raid sirens wailed through the depths of the Antarctic winter. Two of their favourite words were "juez" and "loco": judge and crazy. The latter word was accompanied by a forefinger against the temple twisted corkscrew-like. The logic went thus: the judge has condemned you; the judge has condemned us; the judge is crazy; therefore we are all victims of a crazy judge. It suited me to go along with this theory. When a prisoner was released, which tended to happen unexpectedly, since most of the prisoners had no legal representation and no idea what was happening to their cases, the cry of "Libertad" (Freedom) reverberated around the jail, and we all rushed to congratulate the lucky recipient of the release papers and share his joy as he hurriedly collected his belongings and walked out through the heavy iron gate. But it was not necessarily the last we saw of them. One young man whose joy we shared was called Angel Roberto Sansul. The following day he was back. The thermal suit he was wearing was covered in mud. We had given him some money, but he said that it had gone on eating and drinking, mostly drinking. He had spent a very uncomfortable night as he had nowhere to sleep, it was pouring with rain and he had been caught in the black-out. He had been allowed back in the prison to dry out, and would be freed again at 6 am the next day. However, I was less sympathetic to him later when Barrozo told us he had been imprisoned for raping an 11-year-old girl. After committing the crime he had shaved his head and starved himself in the hope that nobody would recognise him. Sometimes a prisoner thought he was due to be freed, and then nothing happened. Humbert, the Chilean who had rolled the apples towards us on our first night, was due to be freed. He put on his best blue shirt and waited all day but nobody came. The next day he became more and more agitated. He paced up and down the corridor and rattled the bars of the outer gate muttering to himself "Finito Pacienca". He was still there when we left. The system was confusing. Some prisoners were "presunto", which meant they were being processed; others were "condemnado", but did not know when they had been condemned. Another prisoner, Ullman, showed me a cutting from a magazine about a prisoner who had been held for eleven years and then found innocent. George, the interpreter, said it was not uncommon for someone to wait for three years and then be given a two-year sentence.

The inmates were a mixed bunch of criminals, mostly local, with one or two more serious offenders among them. Chileans easily fell foul of the local police, and there was a small group of them in the prison. With the Chilean border being only a few miles away, there was a Chilean minority in Ushuaia, and as Chile and Argentina were traditional enemies they were often picked on by the local police. Even if they had committed no crime, if their documents were not in order and they had no money, they were put in jail. Normally there were around 26 prisoners in the single row of 12 cells that formed the prison, which meant that some were sharing. One or two of the prisoners were long term "condemned" men, who had been found guilty, and they tended to have their own cells. Humbert was one, and he had decorated the walls of his cells with large paintings of sailing ships, all in blue. The rest were being processed (presunto), like us.

The most serious offender was Chino, who was serving a sentence for grievous bodily harm and robbery – eight million pesos, which sounded a lot. But with an exchange rate of 15,000 pesos to the dollar that made only 500 dollars, which sounded less impressive. He did not know how long his sentence was for. He had the names of his two daughters tattooed on his arms, one on each wrist. Next to the name "Alexandria", aged 8, was a cross. He explained that she was dead. He claimed to have been tortured into a confession. He was surprisingly sensitive, and as the war raged on he became depressed at the loss of life on both sides. "Christ does not exist," he kept saying. "God is unjust." But he was extremely unrealistic about life on the outside. I wrote in my diary: "He keeps asking me about the price of greyhounds in Britain, about which I have no idea. He has a scheme for me to buy them and send them to him to race in Bahia Bianca. He says he would make a lot of money and forward all the winnings to me. He says greyhound racing is less corrupt than horse-racing because there are no jockeys to slow down the dogs."

Then there was a large Uruguayan called Castro, the only big-time criminal, who was inside for some sort of terrorist offence. I later learned that he had belonged to the Tupamaros, a Uruguayan urban guerrilla group that went in for kidnappings and assassinations, including the kidnapping of a British ambassador, Geoffrey Jackson. He had served five years in Uruguay, and given the brutal repression of the Tupamaros by the Uruguayan military he was lucky to be alive. He was addicted to Olivia Newton-John, and played her music very loud all day. Castro was in the next cell to us, and we knew immediately he was awake because of the blast of Olivia Newton-John music from his cell.

The most pathetic prisoner was Rocky Moreno, aged 25, who had a permanent limp and was rather slow mentally. He was serving two years for hitting an officer with his rifle during his national service. He clung to us, followed us around like a pet dog, and said we were the only friends he had ever had. He was very good at practical things, such as fixing electric lights with bits of copper wire, or getting an electric fire going. He had been brought up in a circus, and confided that he had had sex only once, and that was with the wife of a lion tamer. Before I was called for interrogation he gave me a small crucifix and a heart which he had made from copper wire.

Then there was Ullman. He was a remarkable man, never dejected, and a natural leader. He was always the one who organised the sharing out of the prison food to ensure everyone got their fair share. He had two platinum pins in his buttocks, and could not open his legs wide. He pushed down his underpants and showed me the cavities. He had had polio as a child and had walked on all fours until he was eleven when the pins were inserted. He was a marvellous mimic, and I can still recall his pretend horse race commentaries using a spoon for a microphone. I know from the speed of delivery and the crescendo that they were brilliant even though I didn't understand a word. He stood for solidarity among the prisoners. He told me we had nothing to fear from the other prisoners. Outside things might be different. "But," and he pointed to the bars, "These bars make us all equal. They throw us together. One person has no power. But here there are 15 of us together and that gives us strength." On the other hand, he could not resist bullying new prisoners who did not know what was what in the prison. In his cell he kept a camouflaged jacket and a baseball cap, which he would put on and then emerge barking orders at them as though he was a prison official. He would order them to hop frog-like up and down the corridor to the great amusement of the other prisoners. I confess I joined in the hilarity. Yet he suffered great pain without complaining, and unlike other prisoners, who were always in and out of the local hospital, he never went for any treatment. One evening he bent over to open the door of the ping-pong room, and had to pull hard because it had been wedged against the strong winds with newspaper. He hobbled away along the corridor in excruciating agony and went to bed. The next day he was still in pain, massaging his leg against the warmth of a radiator.

There was also a quiet little Chilean, who was forever washing himself. One day he told me he was in prison for cattle smuggling. He said that cows cost twice to three times as much in Chile as in Argentina. So he simply drove them across the border, until he was caught. Another prisoner, Pinto, told me he had met an English girl, Susan Johnson, in Punta Arenas, and had fallen in love. He had written her a letter in Spanish, and asked me to translate it into English, which I did with the aid of a dictionary. It was a rather sad letter that began: "Estimada Amiga Susan" and went on to apologise for not having written because for the whole of the previous year he had been "in obscurity". He didn't want her to know that he was in prison. His crime had had something to do with forged documents, and apparently his name was not Pinto. According to Barrozo, he had wandered around Peru, Ecuador, Chile and Argentina, using different names for some reason. But there was a coincidence. For two years he had been a waiter at the Cabo de Hornos Hotel in Punta Arenas, and had been working there in November 1978 when I stayed there.

One inmate who puzzled me was Antonio. A short squat youth of around 20, he wore a shiny maroon smoking jacket and black tie, and waited on the prison officers by day, returning to the cells to sleep. From time to time he would approach us with dollar bills he wanted changing into Argentine money. One day he arrived in a panic, and asked us to tell the prison authorities that we had given him 20 dollars. Apparently, he had been caught stealing. He crossed his wrists to indicate he could be incarcerated for longer. All of a sudden, all the prisoners, including the three of us, were herded into the dining room and our cells were searched. One million pesos had gone missing from the bedroom of one of the prison officers. I saw Antonio's bedding in a pile in a corner. The next morning I found him sitting on his bed staring at the ground, stripped of his smoking jacket and tie and wearing a tee-shirt. He had been found guilty and summarily condemned to two more years. He was a waiter at the Canal Beagle Hotel, and had been only a few days from the end of an eight-month sentence. Forward-thinking was not the strong point of the other prisoners. I felt sorry for him, but he had always struck me as a bit shifty. When I discussed the situation with the night duty officer he said that Antonio was "rapido", which sounded like the right adjective to me.

The number of prisoners was swollen at the weekends by the Saturday night drunks. They were put together in a large cell at the end of the corridor. There was a pile of foam rubber in the corner from which emanated a smell of stale human bodies and urine. I began to recognise the same characters. They would be brought in after midnight on a Friday, locked in the drunks' cell for the weekend, taken before the judge on Monday morning, fined the equivalent of 50 pence and set free. The next weekend as often as not they were back. Then there was the women's section, which was round the corner from our corridor, and separated by a metal gate. One day Commander Grieco took us to see it. There were two cells with one woman in each. "This is where you go if you are really good boys," Grieco joked. A young woman sitting on the floor in the corner of one cell with a towel draped around her flashed a smile. She was Maria, aged 22, officially a dancer called Carina, in fact a prostitute in a local night club called The Igloo. She was in prison for two years for hitting another woman with a broken bottle, taking out her eye. Grieco said later that prostitution was virtually a respectable profession in Ushuaia, and that a number of the wives of important people, including the governor himself, had been prostitutes. This theory seemed confirmed when I met Maria again ten years later. But more of that anon. The other woman was a pathetic case. Rosa was in prison for killing her 13th baby. Infanticide is a common offence in Argentina, a Roman Catholic country. Yet there is little sympathy for the desperate women who commit the crime. During our stay Rosa was transferred to a prison in Buenos Aires for psychiatric treatment. She was very unhappy in her new surroundings, and wrote a desperate appeal to Barrozo asking him if she could come back to Ushuaia. But we never saw her again.

The most common form of fantasising among the prisoners was about sex. A large clandestine sex manual with coloured illustrations, which was apparently permitted in the prison because it was "medical" was passed around constantly, and our fellow inmates would helpfully point to the illustrations and say "fucky fucky" with relish. One evening I described how, on an assignment in Afghanistan after the Soviet invasion I had seen a peasant having intercourse with a donkey while the creature placidly carried on eating grass, its tail over his left shoulder. Not to be outdone, one of the prisoners described a similar adventure with a pig. He had tucked the animal's hindquarters down the front of his Wellington boots. Yet when we discussed our own dreams we discovered that most were about food, although Tony had had one about escaping, with the Chilean prisoners helping him across the Beagle Channel in a coracle.

The shout of "Comida" heralded the arrival of each of the two meals a day we were given. The food was adequate, but basic. My least favourite dish was chickens' necks, which usually appeared at the weekend. The worst aspect for me was that prisoners were not allowed to have eating utensils because of the danger of fights and suicides. They all ate with their hands, seated around a large oblong table in the common room. However, the sight of prisoners "mucking in" with gravy running down their fingers put me off my food. I wrote: "I remember once at a lamb feast in Amman in Jordan watching guests in expensive suits roll up a sleeve, tear off large piece of lamb and eat it with their fingers. I stood in a corner averting my eyes, and was the only guest using a knife and fork." Eventually, we were allowed to take our plates to our cells if we wished, and that is what I did. Fortunately, the Sunday Times and Observer reporters who managed to get in to see us brought us some money, which Barrozo agreed to keep in his safe. So we were able to send out for food. At first none of the prison officers would agree to shop for us, apparently on patriotic grounds. But as time went by and personal relations improved several of them were willing. We stacked up with large bars of chocolate, and also with toilet paper, which was non-existent in the prison. The other prisoners were envious not of the chocolate but of the toilet paper, and often asked us for a piece, which we usually gave them.

We also handed out chocolate from time to time, but occasionally some of the prisoners would help themselves. Once a large bar of chocolate went missing, and my suspicions fell on Castro, the large Uruguay. I confronted him in his cell, and he denied the charge. But he was not the brightest prisoner in the building, and the large bar was protruding from his pocket as he had neglected to hide it.

There was nearly always tension beneath the surface, and from time to time it erupted in fights among the prisoners. One broke out between Humbert and Salis. According to Humbert, it started when Salis objected to Humbert's dancing in the corridor to loud music. Humbert said he had been trying to cheer himself up. I did not witness it, but I saw the result. Both men were given three days isolation, and their cell doors remained firmly locked during that period. Another time Rocky burst into the TV room scowling, broke the leg off a metal chair and wrapped a piece of chain around it and went out into the corridor. We heard crashing and shouting, and the prisoner officers rushed in. Rocky claimed that he had lost his cool after being ragged by a Chilean for spending too much time in bed. He said that because of tension in his head he had not been able to stop himself from lashing out. On June 4 I wrote: "Never a dull moment. The day begins with yet another fight, this time involving virtually all the other prisoners. There is fighting with chair legs, the usual weapons of choice in this place, and blood is smeared on a cell wall. The guards rush in, and all the prisoners are herded into the dining room. Tony is called as a witness. Later they want to know what we have had stolen from our cell, and to whom we have given cigarettes. In fact, we have had stolen a bar of chocolate, a bar of peanut butter, some sugar and some cigarettes (Gauloise). They found a packet of cigarettes outside the bathroom window. The investigation continues."

A few days later details of the "castigation" of the pugilists emerged. No TV and no yerba maté - a local drink - for all of them for four days. In addition, Castro, Salis and Humbert were deprived of their heaters for 30 days. One consequence was a procession of people knocking on our cell door wanting to light their cigarettes on our heater. I was told by the other prisoners that there were strict punishments for breaches of the rules. If anyone was caught smuggling alcohol into the prison they were put into what the prisoners called "The Submarine" for ten days. This was a small room next to cell number one with no windows and no bed. The prisoner lived in total darkness and ate meals in the dark. No one was subjected to this punishment during my stay. But the "Submarine" was sometimes used to provide a temporary bed for people who found themselves homeless for the night. Late that night we watched "The Enemy Below" in the TV room. Three of the prisoners crept in to watch, though they were supposed to be banned. Suddenly the siren went, and Ullman dressed only in striped briefs, his eyes bulging like a frog's, appeared in the doorway in a panic. He switched off the lights, thinking it was an air raid. We told him it was only a fire siren as a message had appeared on the TV screen telling the local fire chief to report for duty. The next day we tried to watch tennis from Paris, but the screen went dead. One of the prisoners translated the explanation. There was a "journalistic problem in London". The transmission was via the UK, and the British had pulled the plug.

CHAPTER SIX
THE WAR COMES TO USHUAIA

By now the whole of Argentine Tierra Del Fuego had been declared a war zone, and all movement was severely restricted. We were told that thick curtains had been hung across airport windows in southern Argentina so that no one could observe military aircraft as we had done. Philip Hayden, a BBC TV reporter and John Thorne, a BBC radio reporter, both colleagues I knew, were ordered to leave Ushuaia. Cal McCrystal was at first allowed to stay as "moral support" for us as we had no visitors. But he was allowed to leave his hotel only to go to the prison or the Police Chief's office or on short diversions for shopping. Then he too was told to return to Buenos Aires. In Ushuaia all phone calls to and from Tierra Del Fuego were now under military control. We were isolated. Then, out of the blue, on Tuesday April 27 I was summoned to the outer office, where there was a phone lying on a desk. I picked it up, and to my astonishment it was Margaret. She had gone into The Observer office and asked for the use of a desk and a phone. She got to work, and after a great deal of effort and ingenuity she managed to get through to the prison. Her first words were: "What in the world are you doing there?" I don't recall much else except that she said she was at The Observer office, and had got through after much effort. When eventually the prison number rang out and someone answered, she said "esposa" (wife) and gave my name. The voice at the other end simply said: "Momento", and within a few minutes she was talking to me. I can't recall much of the conversation except my saying something about it being nothing to worry about and that it would all blow over. She told me she was in touch with the partners of the other two. She was the first person from the outside world to phone the prison and speak to any of us. An amazing achievement, but if anybody could have done it, it was her. In my diary I wrote: "It was wonderful to hear her voice, and she was so positive. She is brilliant in crises, and is going to be so over the next weeks/months/years, however long it takes. I think it was Edward Behr (of Newsweek), author of "Anyone here Been Raped and Speaks English", who said that good journalists' wives were like gold dust and should be cherished. How fortunate I am."

Eventually, a Swiss diplomat, Werner Ballmer, made it to Ushuaia on behalf of the British embassy, for whom the Swiss Government was acting. Even with diplomatic status it had taken him two days to reach Ushuaia from Buenos Aires because of military restrictions on movement in the South. He had had to travel into Chile and out again by road. He went to see the judge, and successfully argued that as we had no visitors we should be allowed to receive telephone calls on humanitarian grounds, provided they were from our three partners and that there was no discussion about the conflict or of anything political. Bob Lowe, a Spanish-speaking journalist at The Observer, gave Margaret enough basic words for her to ask for me – esposa, marido etc. The system worked, though in Margaret's first call a hostile disembodied voice began telling us in English to stop talking after only five minutes. Margaret often found it hard to get through on the phone. In those days calls had to be booked via an international operator in London, who called the operator in Buenos Aires. The Argentine operators refused to accept calls from Britain. But they had no way of knowing where the calls were coming from. One operator got round the problem by putting on an Australian accent, and announcing: "Sydney calling". Another pretended to be Irish, and told them in an Irish accent that Dublin was calling. The ruse worked. It was from Margaret that I heard for the first time of the campaign that was about to be organised by the two newspapers on our behalf. Its slogan was "Free The Ushuaia Three", and posters were being printed to be

Judy Winchester, Margaret and Hilary Holden at the launch of the "Free the Journalists" campaign

displayed in offices and homes. Its chairman was Garret Fitzgerald, former Prime Minister of Ireland, a shrewd choice because Ireland was Roman Catholic, like Argentina, and a member of the European Union so could bring some of the EU's clout into play. We were fortunate that Garret had the time to spare. The launch was to be at the Hilton in London, and the list of supporters included every editor in Fleet Street, and the editors of The New York Times, Washington Post, Boston Globe, Le Monde, La Stampa and many others.

Later I heard that at the launch "the girls looked stunning and said their bit". I don't think anyone would put it like that nowadays, but it evoked exactly the right sort of image for me at the time. The press conference got coverage on the BBC, ITN and in almost all the newspapers. ITN went to Simon's house and filmed his children and his computer, which the reporter described as "silent". The two newspapers also hired William Rodgers, formerly President Jimmy Carter's Secretary for Latin American Affairs, to work his South American contacts in Washington. Margaret told me over the phone

Ian Mather; Tony Prime (Observer), Simon Winchester (Sunday Times)
at police headquarters in Ushuaia.

The Campaign Poster

that Rodgers, Willy Balaban, our lawyer and Anthony Whittaker, The Sunday Times lawyer, had had dinner at the house of Robert Chesshyre, Washington correspondent of The Observer, to plan our defence. They had taken a lot of material from London, including weighty volumes of Jane's Fighting Ships and Jane's All the World's Aircraft to demonstrate that the details in my notebooks had all been published before. Reporters on newspapers worldwide were briefed, and the campaign ensured that no Argentine minister anywhere in the world could hold a press conference without being asked a question about us. Lobbying was carried out at the highest level. Hugo Young of the Sunday Times, who was a confidant of Cardinal Basil Hume, head of the Roman Catholic Church in England and Wales, said that Hume had given the Pope a full brief about our situation as the Pope was due to visit Argentina. When Cal McCrystal went to Dublin to write about the Irish initiative at the United Nations, Charles Haughey, the Prime Minister, asked to see him. He said the Irish would take up our case with the Argentines at the UN. Raymond Carr, my Modern History tutor at New College, Oxford, now Warden of St Anthony's, had written to Nicanor Costa Mendez, the Argentine Foreign Minister, who was a benefactor of St Anthony's, asking for my release. Walter Cronkite, the hugely respected American news anchor, had contacted the Argentine justice and foreign ministers on behalf of the Committee to Protect Journalists. King Juan Carlos of Spain was preparing to intervene. The big guns of the world of journalism were also brought into play. The New York Times, Washington Post and Los Angeles Times all ran editorials calling for our release. In a leader the New York Times said: "There is a wiser way for Argentina to show its displeasure with Fleet Street: three one-way tickets to London." There were stories in the world's press about us almost every day.

Our wives too became TV and radio stars, appearing on BBC current affairs programmes, especially the Today programme on Radio 4. Margaret accepted an invitation from the Today programme to go into Broadcasting House and use her weekly phone call to me to ask if I was willing to be interviewed. I replied that provided she

Crying 'Spy' in Argentina

Argentines don't like their country to be portrayed as brutal and lawless, a place where justice is arbitrary and prisons are horrible. But those are pretty good descriptions of what the Argentine junta has done to three accredited British journalists: slammed them into tiny cells, denied them bail and charged them with espionage.

Understandably, given the frenzy over the Falklands, Argentina is jumpy about the apparent snoopiness of these reporters from London, Simon Winchester of The Sunday Times and Ian Mather and Tony Prime, of The Observer. They were initially arrested on April 13 for behaving suspiciously — they were taking notes and asking questions — at an Argentine military base in Tierra del Fuego.

What passes understanding is why Argentina is now so determined to throw the book at the three. If for doing their job these Britons are given long sentences, Argentina adds to its reputation for savagery, and weakens its own argument that 1,800 Falklanders would be well-treated under Argentine law. There is a wiser way for Argentina to show its displeasure with Fleet Street: three one-way tickets to London.

New York Times editorial comment, 29 April 198

A few of the hundreds of news stories from around the world

and no one else asked the questions there could be no objection since there was nothing in the rules to say that our conversation could not be broadcast. I also suggested that we should do it immediately before the Argentines realised what was happening and decided to pull the plug. The interview was broadcast the next morning, and I was able to describe my daily life in the prison, including playing table tennis, and standing on a chair in the cell and pretending to walk along the tops of the mountains. Afterwards an impressed Today producer jokingly asked Margaret if she wanted a job. There were newspaper interviews, too, in which she tried to divert the reporters away from what she called the "sob story" angle and to concentrate on the "Free the Ushuaia Three" campaign. "I don't want a story about the agony of the wife who waits", she told one reporter. The result was inevitable. She opened the newspaper to find herself gazing at the headline: "Agony of the Wife who Waits". After years of being married to a journalist she kicked herself for having given them the very headline she didn't want. People from all walks of life sent letters to the Argentine justice ministry or the Argentine foreign ministry, in English or in Spanish. This was still the era of telegrams, and the judge alone received more than 600 of them demanding our release. Earlier he had insisted that we were spies, but now under this bombardment he told us irritably and also a little defensively: "I know you are journalists. But I have to find out what you have discovered." One afternoon as it was going dark, the full impact of all that was being done on our behalf suddenly overwhelmed me. I went into the silent deserted dining room, crossed to the window, gripped the bars, stared long and hard at the grimy glacier now deep in shadow across the road and bit my lip to stop the tears of gratitude.

We now had virtually no visitors. One or two journalists, however, managed to hang on in Tierra Del Fuego for a while, and one even persuaded Commander Grieco to let him see us in prison. James Brooke of the Miami Herald wrote an excellent article about the mood in Ushuaia, and he was good enough to smuggle out letters from us to our families. He described me as: "a veteran Third World newsman with a reputation for going to nasty places to get difficult stories". For the journalists in Buenos Aires life was also frustrating. By now they were banned from travelling anywhere in Argentina and largely confined to the Sheraton Hotel. They whiled away their time playing six-a-side football in the hotel gymnasium. I was informed that the French were the champions, mainly through a player who gained the nickname Exocet for the deadly accuracy of his shooting. Every journalist except one (Time magazine on the grounds that it would be taking sides in the conflict) signed a petition asking for our release, and the list was displayed on a large board in the hotel. One or two reporters did make attempts to dodge the restrictions, but came to grief. One day when I was watching the lunchtime TV I saw Julian Manyon, a Thames TV reporter, being interviewed. The previous day he and the camera crew had left the hotel to film in the street and had been abducted. They had been found six hours later standing by a road naked, having been robbed of clothes, money and cameras. President Galtieri visited them at the hotel to issue a personal apology. The episode did at least reveal how sensitive the Argentine Junta was over its international reputation in the aftermath of the Dirty War. That, at least, was a bit of good news from our point of view. Another group of journalists was based in Punta Arenas, the nearest Chilean town. They were also kicking their heels while being regularly rebuffed in their efforts to cross into Argentine Tierra Del Fuego. They were all staying at the Cabo de Hornos Hotel, and sent us a good wishes card, which they had all signed. The hotel manager had added at the bottom: "I'd swap you for this lot any day."

My knowledge about the progress of the war varied greatly throughout my time in prison. By now the British task force had managed to land undetected on the west coast of the Falklands, and was trudging (the British called it "yomping") its way towards Port Stanley, the capital. I knew the outlines of what was going on, although at the time I had no way of knowing what an extraordinary military feat it was proving to be. Nor did I know that the Argentines had no practicable plan for defending the Falklands. But it was becoming obvious to me that the various court hearings and appeals relating to my case and the cases of my two colleagues, were inextricably entwined with events in the Falklands War, although the Argentines would never admit it. So there was every reason to try to keep up with the news as best we could. At times I was dependent on the Argentine media. In the communal dining room was a black-and-white TV set, which was usually on during the day. Periodically, there would be loud martial music, a hand bearing a flaming torch would appear on the screen, and a deep masculine voice would announce an impending communiqué from the Casa Rosada, the Presidential palace. Prisoners and warders alike rushed to the TV room. At first the announcements were mostly fantasy, consisting of hugely exaggerated numbers of British planes shot down and warships sunk. There was also an incessant accompanying militaristic jingle; "Vamos Argentinos. Vamos A Vencer".- Let us go, Argentines. Let us go and win, which accompanied a shot of Argentines shown gazing reverentially upwards at the pale blue and white Argentine flag. Each communiqué had a number, and by the end of the fighting the total was well over 100. The Argentine press fanned the militaristic mood. I remember in particular a magazine called Siete Dias (Seven Days). The front cover was divided horizontally in two. The top half showed a group of British soldiers leaning over the side rail of the cruise ship Canberra, which had been requisitioned as a troop carrier, as it left Portsmouth for the Falklands, waving bras on sticks. The caption said: "For Money". The bottom half showed a row of determined young Argentine conscripts in a trench, and the caption said: "For Country". The message was that the British troops were mercenaries (because they were professionals), while the Argentine soldiers (who were conscripts) were patriots.

May 3 was a black day. I first suspected that something significant had happened when the Chilean inmates, who had never made any secret about being on the side of the British, started making noises like falling bombs, followed by explosions, then ""glug glug glug", and finally loud cheers. Tony was on the phone to Hilary, his partner, when the phone was suddenly snatched from him, he was pushed against a wall and hustled back to the cell. Argentina had announced that its cruiser, the General Belgrano, with 1,000 men on board, had been torpedoed and must be presumed sunk. It looked like the loss of life would be huge. To make things even worse from our point of view, the doomed vessel had sailed from Ushuaia (on April 26 accompanied by two destroyers). Ushuaia was a naval town, and the mood of the whole population would be grim. I had just been listening to Philip Knightley, Sunday Times journalist and author of the classic book on war reporting, "The First Casualty", talking on the BBC about truth and propaganda. He said that journalists who were adventurous in reporting wars could find themselves in prison charged with spying "as has happened to three of our colleagues". At least we belonged to the more respectable branch of the trade of journalism, I smugly said to myself. But that night the cell door burst open, the lights were switched on and a group of prison officers swooped.. They grabbed books we had collected, radio and food. In my diary, which I kept under the bed, I wrote: "Tonight home seems not only miles but years away. I simply cannot see any speedy and happy ending to this nightmare." Later I wrote: "Around 11 pm Bulletin 19. 128 survivors, which means over 800 dead. The lights fused, and we were plunged into darkness. Listened to a tape of Chariots of Fire". In the end, 770 men were rescued and 323 killed. The bodies were brought back to Ushuaia, and Grieco was in charge of receiving them. The General Belgrano had been hit by two torpedoes from the British submarine Conqueror. The sinking was hugely controversial in Britain as well as throughout the world, as technically the cruiser was outside the 200-mile Exclusion Zone announced by Britain, and was sailing away from the Falklands.

The next morning, we were informed that our "privileges" were to be taken away immediately i.e. all written material except that in Spanish. The guards came into the cell, and systematically removed all remaining books. Fortunately, they did not touch my diary. I had decided to try and kick up a fuss on the grounds that it was as "personal" as my tooth brush or socks. Our money was also taken off us, so we could no longer buy any extras. We were also informed that we would not be allowed to receive any more phone calls. All visitors had to be authorised by the judge, and an interpreter had to be present all the time. My low spirits led to an even worse loss of appetite. I wrote: "At lunch I try to cut a piece of meat with a spoon. Opposite is a poor grey-haired old lag eating with his fingers. I shade my eyes so that I cannot see the others eating, but I have no appetite and only just stop myself from throwing up". The next night was no better: "Tonight's dinner was ghastly. Watching these people guzzle inedible food with their hands takes away all my appetite." But I did develop the habit of hoarding pieces of bread, as we were given nothing to eat between 8 pm and lunch the next day.

In the early weeks of our captivity we worked together as a team, calling committee meetings to discuss the latest developments, including the significance, if any, of minor spats among the other prisoners. The idea of calling a meeting when you are all locked in the same cell now seems weird. But it helped me to realise that while we may have been helpless in some ways, we were powerful in others. We decided we should prepare ourselves to exploit any opportunities that arose. Simon and I decided to learn Spanish. We spent hours sitting opposite each other on our bunks, reading words out of a Spanish dictionary for the other one to guess. Simon seemed to be better at nouns, while I understood verbs. We made good progress and soon we could have a reasonable conversation with prison officials and other prisoners if they spoke slowly. I could understand most of the news in Spanish, and I became a fan of an afternoon programme for children fronted by a bearded character called "Father Argentina", who told simple stories and began each programme with "Hola, chicos. Qué tal?" Hello little ones. How are you? Tony, however, made no effort to learn Spanish. He did not even know the Spanish word for "twenty", and thought that "Che passa?" meant cup. He said he had a mental blockage about languages, but managed to communicate with the other inmates without any problems.

Our linguistic struggles were now rewarded. When the General Belgrano was sunk we decided to write a note to Barrozo. Although we had been stripped of reading material during the night it had been decided that we could keep anything written in Spanish. So we used a Spanish edition of Readers Digest to help us compose a letter to Barrozo stating that while we remained British patriots we were personally deeply saddened by the loss of life and the distress of the families of those killed. Barrozo later told us he had been moved by our letter. A few days later the Argentines sank the British guided missile destroyer, HMS Coventry, a terrible blow to Britain. We decided to write another note using the same copy of Readers Digest to find the right words. The aim was to try to neutralise the hostility towards us that had developed as a result of the sinking of General Belgrano. We said that just as we had felt sympathy for those who had lost their lives on the General Belgrano we hoped the Argentine authorities would understand that we felt exactly the same over the deaths of our compatriots on the Coventry. It paid off. Barrozo invited us into his office, where he offered us Argentine whisky, which he pronounced "Wikky", called "Old Smuggler", pronounced with a heavy "u" just as Lancashire people pronounce "bus". From then on our relationship with him became not only thoroughly professional, but also at times cordial.

Spanish was not the only language we learned. As we continued to build relationships within the prison the other prisoners taught us "Lunfardo", slang associated with criminals. The basic principle is that the syllables of word are reversed, so that "casa" (house) becomes "saca", "vacca" (cow), "cava" "mucher" (woman") "chermu". Not very subtle. There are special words for "policeman" – "boton", and "police" in general – "yuta". There is a wonderful criminal word for "danger, police present" – "wananaya", pronounced with the "aya" at the end elongated, as though it were an Italian lament. This word is to be accompanied by a stroking of the right side of the nose with a forefinger to confirm its authenticity. The prisoners told me that I was particularly privileged to be given this inside information, and that I must not divulge it to anyone. Just before I left Ushuaia I asked Barrozo if he knew the criminal sign for "secret police are present". Of course, he said, stroking his nose. Every detective here knows that!"

I had begun to settle down. In my diary I wrote: "An interesting feature of prison life is the amount of pretending that is normal among the prisoners. One prisoner, Ullman, an armed robber, is always pretending to be a sports commentator or an opera singer. Rocky, our devoted friend, in jail for hitting an officer while doing his National service, takes his dog for an imaginary walk along the corridor." Simon and I also went for long walks along this passage, which was 25 or so spaces long, pretending that we were rambling in the country. The shower at the end was a waterfall. The other cells, where gourds of yerba maté, the local version of tea drunk through a metal straw, were usually being brewed on upended electric fires, were cafés conveniently situated along the route.

My life was now dominated by prison routine. "Arriba" (Get up) accompanied by the tapping of the night warden's keys on the cells doors heralded the start of the day, followed by "Forma", when we stood in line outside our cells doors, and responded to our names. Each prisoner would shout "Presente". Occasionally there was a silence, and eventually a faint "Presente" would come from the direction of the lavatory. After that there was nothing to do except for those prisoners who were on kitchen duty or allocated to work at the local hospital. Some prisoners spent a lot of time sitting on their beds staring at the ground, and other prisoners would approach them and say "aburrido?" – bored. It was one of the first Spanish words I learned. Some did physical exercise with chest expanders. Humbert concentrated on painting sailing ships. For me, there were a couple of ways round the boredom problem. We had a number of books, and I forced myself to read even those I did not particularly want to read. Two women, Jane Scotti and Marghuerita Vasquez, the former British and the latter Argentine, would visit us from time to time. Marghuerita was the interpreter from the court. Her husband had been manager of a local centolla factory, but had left to become

The author in prison, drawn by Margaret from her imagination

a sociologist working for the Tierra Del Fuegan Government on problems of social welfare, of which there were many. Ushuaia had a large transient population. Most of the population worked for government agencies on contracts of a year or two, and few stayed longer. Others arrived from the North mistakenly believing Tierra Del Fuego was Elderado because gold had once been found there, but they soon got into trouble as there was little work. Then there were those who stayed because they had reached the end of the South American Highway, and had nowhere to go except back. There was a saying that only the mad, the bad and the sad lived in Tierra Del Fuego.

Jane Scotti was formerly Jane Wood from Birmingham, now married to an Argentine. Both women were devoted to the Argentine cause over the "Malvinas", but felt sorry for us as we had no visitors. They brought us books, and a chess set which had a basic computer. One visit was ended abruptly by an air raid warning, and we were herded back to our cell. After 20 minutes or so the all-clear sounded. I tried the chess set, and played a few times, then had to give up. When you made a wrong move a red light came on, and the computer emitted a jingle that became increasingly irritating. At first I set the computer to number five, the most difficult on its scale. Then as I lost I reduced it to four and then three. Increasingly I became convinced that the computer declared a wrong move on my part only when it was losing. So I gave up chess. However, I flourished at table tennis. I had played it as a teenager in the social club at the Baptist chapel I had attended, and found I still took to the game naturally. There was a table tennis table in the common room, and no shortage of opponents among the other prisoners and the prison staff. My only rule was that when playing doubles we should try to avoid England against Argentina, or England and Chile together against Argentina in case tempers flared. The Chileans in the prison were passionately pro-British, and cheered every Argentine loss, whether in the war or at table tennis. One was mildly embarrassing, the other disturbing.

I read everything that came to hand – Harold Robbins for the first time, and Sophocles for the second, since I had once done some political philosophy at university plus any Argentine newspapers I could get hold of. I also found small ways of spinning out the most elementary tasks. I would walk to the bathroom to wash, walk back to the cell, linger for a few minutes, then pick up my toothpaste and make a second journey to the bathroom. I would wash my sheets in cold water and dry them over the electric fire a section at a time. With a bit of skill this job could be made to stretch out for most of a day. Practising Spanish by talking to the other prisoners also passed the time, and I had to keep consulting a large Spanish Larousse. What I did not realise was that I was learning to speak with a Tierra Del Fuegan accent. This has a touch of Scottish about it, and the letter 'r' is heavily pronounced. The local TV evening news was called "Micro Noticias", and was read by two dour individuals, who spoke of "Rrrrio Grrrande" and "Rrrossarrrio". "Rio Gallegos" was pronounced "Rrrio Gajeagos" with a French "je" in the middle, and not Rio Gayegos as in European Spanish. We joked about British news readers saying: "the carrr brrrroke thrrrrough the barrrierrrr" Well, it amused us at the time! Just before we left I watched King Juan Carlos of Spain opening the football World Cup in Madrid on TV, and wondered why he spoke in such a peculiar accent.

I wrote in my diary for May 3 that a prison officer came into our cell and took away a small table. We decided to stop the rot, and sent a note to Barrozo in Spanish once again painstakingly worked out from a dictionary. He said that he had been ordered by Buenos Aires to stop all phone calls to us, but that the judge had decided that the Argentine military did not understand our situation and was standing up to them. So he was prepared to allow us to receive calls of up to five minutes duration. After some negotiation we managed to increase the time, and it was agreed that each of us could receive one call a week of 15 minutes duration between 8pm and 9pm local time, which would be midnight in the UK. One of us would take Sunday, another Tuesday and the third Thursday, and these times would be communicated to our wives. They would be the only ones allowed to call, and they would work out a rota among themselves. There was to be no discussion of the military or political situation, and George, the prison interpreter, would listen in. Margaret chose Thursdays to phone me because she knew it was the best time for getting a story into The Observer based upon what I said. Every week during my captivity The Observer ensured that there was a story about the three of us on its front page. Painstakingly I wrote out the new rules, translated them into Spanish with the aid of a dictionary and some input from a couple of prisoners and sent them to Barrozo. The Comisario replied that we would receive all that we were entitled to, and ordered our table to be returned. As I felt we were on a roll I thought I would see what happened if I asked him if we could have three beers. They duly arrived, and I paid Antonio, the waiter. A satisfactory day's work.

There were some more new arrivals. I was highly amused when an Argentine journalist who had subjected us to hostile questions in the press conference after the judge had decided that we had a case to answer turned up in the prison. He had been arrested for writing an article critical of police arrangements in Tierra Del Fuego. His name was Manuel Bordon, and by now he was friendly enough. We managed to converse in French, and he told me he was a freelance working for "Norte" magazine. He said he had also published the name of the governor of Tierra Del Fuego, which he was not supposed to do as the island was now a military zone. That didn't sound like much of a crime to me. Unfortunately, it did seem to make the behaviour of "The Ushuaia Three" seem rather more serious by comparison. Bordon said he was "at the disposition of the Admiral", which was also revealing since the judge had assured us that Argentine justice was independent of the military, and that he not the military, was in charge. Anyway, I sympathised with Bordon, and told him I didn't think he would be in prison very long. A couple of days later he was gone. Another newcomer was a young sailor who was 18 or 19 years old. He was very nervous, and late at night when there was no one around he approached Tony. He said he had been in the Malvinas, clasped his hands together and said: "Britain Argentina Friends". Then he shook Tony's hand, saluted him smartly and returned to his cell. Another was a Chilean boy accused of robbery. He said: "I 17. I speak English." Then pointing around he said "wall, ceiling, water, fucky fucky". The latter phrase always produced laughter all round. The boy was separated from the rest of us because he was "minoridad" – under 18. Another new arrival was extremely filthy and spent his time sitting at the end of the corridor picking dirt off his feet. I never did find out who he was, and he disappeared from the prison.

As an "old lag" I began to take it upon myself to try to help other prisoners who were having difficulty coping. One such was a smartly-dressed young man with a well-trimmed moustache, who said he had written a cheque for 70 million pesos which had bounced. Apparently, he was from a well-off family, and was accused of forging the cheque. He arrived on a Friday, and when he was told he would have to remain until at least Monday he was beside himself with grief and frustration that his family had not been able to arrange his immediate release. I spent most of the weekend talking to him and making bowls of maté. We played chess and I let him win. Honest I did. On Monday he waited in his best suit and tie to see the judge, but was not called. He said he was a friend of Grieco, and that his time in prison was a disgrace to his family. In his cell he had his own TV set from home, but he spent a lot of time reading the Argentine Penal Code. After a week he was called to see the judge, and freed. I patted him on the back and congratulated him. Not once during the week did he ever show interest in any other prisoner. He never even said goodbye or thank you. This attitude was totally untypical of the prisoners in general. "Give me the morality of the robber or the army deserter any day", I wrote. I found that I was developing an empathy with the other prisoners, despite our very different backgrounds. Of course, I knew them only in prison, and had no direct experience of the crimes of which they were accused. But years later I find I still have an instinctive sympathy with prisoners, whatever they have done.

Occasionally, Barrozo would come into our cell late at night and sit on one of the beds, his walkie-talkie beside him. On June 7 after one such session I wrote: "We discussed a wide range of topics, including the Israeli invasion of Lebanon, and the breathalyzer in Argentina. We then got on to the subject of Maria Carrera, who had been released that day. Barrozo said that she was a prostitute at the Tropicana." This must have been another night club in Ushuaia in addition to The Igloo. I was surprised that Ushuaia could support more than one night club. Barrozo told us that as a detective it was his job to know all the prices – 15 dollars for two hours in Ushuaia. In Buenos Aires they were more expensive because they were "on a higher level" and "bi-lingual". On a more practical note, he left saying that the three of us could have knives for eating our food, provided we hid them under our mattresses so that the other prisoners did not see them. That was great news for me. Unfortunately, the knives did not materialise.

Occasionally, there was a break from the routine. On one occasion Grieco took us to his house, and gave us tea, cakes and dolce de leche, milk caramel. We met his teenage daughters, who had set up a war room in their bedroom. We joked with them about how to pronounce "Argentina", deliberately mispronouncing the "r", so that they shouted out the correct pronunciation time after time to our amusement. It was innocent fun, and showed Grieco to be a humane man as well as a proud Marine. From time to time we were asked by the prison authorities if we would agree to be interviewed by the Argentine or other media, and usually agreed. There were one or two bad results. A particularly annoying example was with the Argentine magazine, Radiolanda 2000. We asked the reporter, whose name was Jorge Omar Irineo, if, in exchange for the interview, he would post short personal notes that we had written to our families. He promised he would, but did no such thing. Instead, he published our rather pathetic notes in the edition of April 23 of the magazine. Would a British journalist have done such a thing? Of course they would! Even so, I wish I could write: "I know where you live, Jorge!" But I don't.

Later Grieco asked us if as a special favour to him we would agree to be interviewed by Venezuelan TV. He warned us they would be hostile as Venezuela supported Argentina in the war, and that we should keep our cool. We were taken to the prison officers' mess in another part of the building, where there was a large gathering of people, many of them in naval uniforms. We were clearly objects of great interest, and were introduced around the room like guests of honour. In my diary I wrote: "In the interview I said that the Falklands/Malvinas crisis could have been solved by diplomacy. The interviewer asked: 'Don't you think 150 years of diplomacy is long enough?' I replied that I personally could see a justification on moral grounds for going to war in self-defence. But I could not see how the Falklands were a threat to Argentina, and I had difficulty in supporting war in pursuit of a territorial claim. I asked what would happen to the world if every country which had a territorial claim were to embark on an invasion in pursuit of its claim. What would the Pope, who was at that moment on his way back to Rome from Argentina , think of that?' Obviously, they would distort the interview if they chose." I never did see the result. After the interview I chatted to a man I assumed was a naval officer. He was wearing a new beautifully-tailored dark blue great coat on top of a naval uniform. A shoulder flash in gold letters said "Corresponsal". He was, in fact, an Argentine radio war reporter. I told him that the only time I had ever worn a uniform had been in Vietnam at the insistence of the Americans, who would not let you anywhere near the front unless you wore military fatigues. Even then I always wore a pair of dull-coloured trousers that were plainly civilian to show I was not a soldier. To do otherwise, I said, would have identified me too closely with the Americans. Unsurprisingly, he said he not been to the Malvinas, and had not seen any of the fighting. On 12 May I wrote: "Through the barred windows I watch the police ceremony (for the 97th anniversary of the founding of the Tierra Del Fuegan police) in the cold light of dawn. They are lined up in their dark blue uniforms in front of Commander Grieco. There is stirring music, and Grieco gives a speech. A photographer is at work among the ranks. If he were to point his camera towards my window he could make himself a small fortune."

As my imprisonment lengthened the days shortened. It came light later and later; dusk began in the early afternoon. The first snow of winter had transformed the landscape, and the brightness hurt my eyes when I stood on a chair in our cell to peer out of the window. I learned to blink rapidly before submitting my eyes to the full glare of the snow-reflected light, which was in such contrast to the perpetual gloom of the prison. I passed some time standing by the window where there was a small stream of fresh cold air to gain some relief from the cigarette smoke. Everyone in the jail smoked except Simon and me, and there was no open air exercise area. Ushuaia was a duty-free port, and cigarettes were only £2 sterling for 200. At first I found it hard to look out of the window because it reminded me too much of freedom. Then I discovered the pleasure of pretending to climb the surrounding mountains in my mind's eye, cheating a little now and then by donning seven-league boots to jump across an obstructive ravine.

On one side of the prison in the distance through the windows I could see the snow-covered mountains of Navarino Island in Chile, which glowed pink at dawn. If I stood on a chair the view was over the wooden roofs of Ushuaia, to the naval dock yard, then the air base, and beyond that the Beagle Channel, on the other side of which were the mountains. This view was south towards Cape Horn and the Antarctic. On some days, especially at weekends, I could see local people ice skating in an inlet of the Beagle Channel known as the Inner Bay. At other times when there were signs of activity, such as aircraft engine noise from across the bay or smoke visible above the roof of the naval dockyard, I would wait to see if any of the Argentine war planes or frigates were about to go into action. Two Argentine frigates were tied up in the dockyard below the prison, and from time to time smoke rose into the air as they started their engines. But they never left port. I assumed that the Argentine Navy was too scared of the Royal Navy, especially the British submarines, and I later discovered that this was correct. Who could blame them? However, one Argentine war ship that did leave port was the cruiser, General Belgrano, which was based in Ushuaia. It left with a large complement of soldiers and sailors, only to be sunk by the British in the most controversial action of the war. Simon later claimed that he had seen it leave. If

Ushuaia runway through the prison bars. The Argentine Air Force hid Skyhawks in the hangar on the right.

that was so he failed to mention it at the time. We were also directly in line with Ushuaia airport and runway, which was used by Argentine Air Force jets, and sometimes saw Skyhawks, which had hidden in a hangar all night, take off then turn east to attack the British fleet. The Argentine Navy also had eight Aermacchi planes which were used for pilot training, and they flew low over the prison roof time after time making a deafening noise as they did touch and go on the runway. We now had far more access to military secrets than we had ever obtained during our abortive mission south from Buenos Aires.

The view through the windows on the other side of the prison was less enticing. I could see a polluted dirt-brown glacier, which ended just across the road, and next to it was a rusting Heath Robinson generating station that clanked and wheezed and belched clouds of white steam when it was operating. The prison was on a corner two blocks up from the waterfront, and the road outside was deep in snow. Ushuaia's roads were on a grid system, and in winter traffic on roads leading to and from the water front had right of way over that on roads running parallel to the waterfront because the steep inclines in the town made stopping and starting quite treacherous. In my diary I wrote: "The water in the shower is so cold it might have come straight from the glacier. It seemed to freeze on my head. But I have decided to shower every day, to keep up standards." I did not always succeed. The shower consisted of a hole in the ceiling to which a tuna fish tin punched with holes had been attached to form a sprinkler rose. There could be a delay of up to ten minutes after you turned on the tap until the first drips of icy water arrived. I would use this time to rub dry soap powder provided by the prison all over my body, and then stand and wait. On more than one occasion no water arrived, and I had to dress again and spend the rest of the day covered in itchy dry soap powder. But when I succeeded my body glowed afterwards.

We still had the occasional visitor to look forward to, usually a journalist who had managed to reach Ushuaia. To my surprise, various press colleagues, whom I had known for years, turned up brandishing brand new Irish passports. At that time it was relatively easy to obtain an Irish passport if you had even the most tenuous connection with Ireland. As Ireland was neutral in the Falklands War and a Catholic country, like Argentina, it was a useful second passport to have, and opened many doors in Argentina. I had no idea so many of my colleagues had Irish grannies. Another country whose passport was welcome was South Africa, which was backing the Argentine cause. George De'ath, a South African TV journalist, was allowed to remain in Ushuaia and was a regular visitor to the prison. Unfortunately, his visits were not all that welcome. George tended to emphasise the negative aspects of our fate. He would inform us about the hostile mood in the town. He spent a lot of time in the officers bar at the Argentine Navy Base in Ushuaia, and once told us he had almost come to blows with officers who had just returned from the Malvinas, who, he said, wanted to tear us to pieces. Poor George was later (June 14 1986) hacked to death with a machete in the Crossroads squatter camp in South Africa during the troubles preceding the surrender of power by the country's whites and the ending of apartheid. But he did his stuff for us. He visited us regularly, and took letters for us which always arrived.

From time to time also there would be what we called a "P. F.D", a potential freedom day, when a court somewhere in Argentina, either local, regional or national, was due to consider some aspect of our case, and could, in theory at least, have ordered our release. We looked forward to these, even though they all ended the same way, as deep down we knew they would. One such was May 31 when the court at Comodoro Rivadavia considered our appeal against refusal of bail. In my diary I wrote: "At 7.30 pm the Comodoro court announced that it had rejected our appeal for bail. It upheld the reasons given by the Ushuaia judge, namely that we are a danger to the security of the state and that there is a danger to us." In one particularly gloomy moment I wondered whether I would be mentally scarred for life. I wrote: "You can be alone when you want to, even in prison; your mind learns to cut out other people. You spend so much time thinking about your own case. Is this healthy, or not? I have no idea what I shall be like when I am released, if and when I ever am. Will I collapse? Will I be normal?" I came to regret writing these words. I used extracts from my diary in an article I wrote for The Observer when I was released. Years later, Adrian Hamilton, deputy editor of The Observer, decided to try to have me sacked from the paper to make way for two of his protegés. He quoted this section at me, and said I might have been psychologically damaged by prison life. Unfortunately for him I was not so damaged that I could not put up a fight. I resisted, the editor backed me and I stayed.

The prison was the most patriotic building in town. When the local TV announced that there would be electricity cut-backs to save energy for the war the prison was the first to "volunteer", and as a result we were without heat or light for hours at a time. The name Tierra Del Fuego, Land of Fire (columns of smoke seen from Indian fires), seemed particularly inappropriate to me then. However, the prison officers quarters were exempt from these restrictions, and on more than one occasion when we were in darkness I recall the officers club being all lit up and the sounds of partying going on late into the night. Local traders also did their patriotic duty. One day the TV station solemnly announced that a local duty-free shop called "London Supply" had changed its name to "Atlantico Sur". (South Atlantic. The store is still there).

Around 3.30 am on the night of May 25, Argentina's National Day, my sleep was disturbed by the sound of people shouting, police sirens and the flickering of light on the cell walls. By this time I had developed a technique for waking up slowly, holding myself in a state of half-consciousness for several minutes, as this made re-entering the real world less brutal. Gradually, as I became fully conscious my first thought was that an angry mob was heading for the prison. Then I realised that the light was caused by flames. I stood on a chair, and looked out of the window. An entire building a couple of hundred yards from the prison, was on fire. Sparks were flying all over the place, and the streets were full of shouting people. The other prisoners were banging on their cells doors, but nobody was taking any notice. Most of the buildings in Ushuaia, including the prison, were made of wood, and the prisoners were all locked in,. We were fortunate that there was little wind that night, and the smoke was billowing along the waterfront and not towards us. Otherwise, the prison could have caught fire. Eventually, the fire burned itself out, and sky visible from my window turned from red to black. The building was the Albatross Hotel, and it was totally destroyed. Some suspected arson, especially as the fire had happened on the night of Argentina's national day. Others said that the electricity had short-circuited. Whatever the cause at least nobody could blame us. George De'ath, the South African journalist, and his cameraman were staying in the hotel, and had fled leaving behind their clothes and cameras. Some guests leapt from the windows naked. Later that day I heard Peter Wilsher, the Sunday Times Foreign Editor, discussing our case on the BBC. He said that all the international pressure had been to no avail and that we were "relying on our spiritual resources."

Towards the end of May I had direct experience of the impact of the MoD's notorious "big lie", about which there is still much argument. There was an excellent evening current affairs show on Argentine TV called "Buenas Noches Argentina", which flew by the seat of its pants with live reports from all over the world. One evening the presenter announced that news had leaked out of London that the British task force did not intend to land in the Malvenas because it would be too dangerous. Instead, the British had decided to impose a "cordon sanitaire" around the islands which, when combined with the bombing of Port Stanley runway, was designed to starve the Argentines into submission. Meanwhile, the British would harass the Argentine defenders with hit and run raids by special forces. The presenter then took a pointer to a map of the Falklands, and announced that that very day there had been British hit-and-run raids "here, here, here, here and here". As he spoke he pointed to five points around the Falklands coast where the British had made raids that day. Yet at that very moment, unknown to the Argentines, the British were carrying out the major disembarkation of the War, the main British force landing undetected at San Carlos Bay. By the time the Argentines found out it was too late as the British had established a bridgehead ashore. In my opinion, which has always remained the same, that lie, put out by Sir Frank Cooper, head of the MoD, was justified because it shortened the war and saved lives. When I got back home none of the other British Defence Correspondents shared my view. Their opinion was that as Defence Correspondents with a special relationship with the MoD they should have been taken into confidence. In fact, they were hoodwinked along with the rest of the media. While the Defence Correspondents were nursing their wounded egos, most of the press – and the public – thought the lie justified. "Fleet Street must have been worth at least three Type-42 destroyers," said my own newspaper, The Observer.

The attitude of the prison staff underwent a transformation as it dawned on them that their government was not telling the truth. They wanted to know what the BBC was saying, so returned the radio that they had confiscated when the General Belgrano was sunk. It was for their benefit rather than ours. We used it to listen to the BBC during the night by opening our cell window a little and poking the radio antenna through the bars. The reception was best at around 2 am because at that time the broadcast was relayed from Ascension Island. As we strained to hear the words it reminded me of one of my earliest memories, trying to listen on a crackling wireless in our terraced house in Preston to reports of the Russians retreating as the Germans advanced towards Moscow. "What does the BBC say?" the prison staff would ask in the mornings, in an overly-casual way, although we knew they were desperate to know. Commander Grieco, however, remained loyal to the Argentine cause. When he learned that the British had landed successfully on the Falklands, he went off to the war room. He returned to express what appeared to be genuine concern for us. "What is happening to your boys on those beaches, terrible," he said "It is Dunkirk all over again." Grieco was proud of the Argentine naval tradition. When the conflict started he had appeared at the door of our cell in full uniform with a white silk cravat. He pointed to the stripe down the side of his trousers, and said that it was a Nelson stripe, just like that of the Royal Navy. He said that the Argentine Navy modelled itself on the Royal Navy. "Now" he announced proudly. "We sail out to confront our teachers in battle." In fact, the Argentine Navy sailed nowhere. After the sinking of the General Belgrano its ships stayed in port. Every day Argentine TV showed the aircraft carrier Veinti Cinco de Mayo ploughing through the waves with Skyhawks taking off from its decks. But it was all library footage, and the same every time. Grieco also told us with great pride that the Argentines were virtually European, unlike the Brazilians and Central Americans. "In this country", he told us proudly, "No niggers. So we are just like you English - racists!" There was widespread disdain in Argentina when the BBC put on special broadcasts in Spanish from Ascension Island. It was pointed out to us that the broadcaster chosen by the BBC had a Mexican accent, which was despised by the racially snobbish Argentines. Not everything I heard on the BBC in the middle of the

Cartoon sent by The Sunday Times

Dear Mr Prime, Mr. Mather and Mr. Winchester.

I am very sorry that you can not be let free to see your family but I am sure you will. Buy the way I am not writing to say talk about that. The other day I went on a trip and I went on the cork screw but I don't think you will of heard of that but it's a carriage witch go up-side-down on a track as there's a big ship witch swing's block and forward.

your's sensealeart
Raymond Duffy.

Letter from a British school child

I still recall those days of you & Tony playing in the sand-pit at Deepdale Council School & running into the shelters when the sirens went
when I heard on the radio the charges made against you I said "never, he's not a boy like that".

Letter from the author's primary school teacher recalling World War II era night was encouraging. I remember listening uneasily to a debate in the House of Commons, in which Tory MPs were baying for the RAF to bomb the Argentine mainland. There we were in a direct line with end of the runway. I remember trying to comfort the others and myself too with a description of modern "smart" bombs that slid down beams with pinpoint precision. If I had known then what I learned later that the bombing of the Port Stanley runway by the RAF's Vulcan bombers was wildly inaccurate I would have slept less easily.

There was also a problem with letters. Many which we knew had been posted to us never reached us. Telegrams, however, came through amazingly quickly, especially if they were addressed properly. As overall boss of the prison and the police Grieco was a stickler for correct names and titles, and he reprimanded us when telegrams arrived addressed to one of us at "El Penitenciario". We explained, probably not very convincingly, that no one wanted to make light of the Argentine penal system, and that they simply did not know the word for "prison". Grieco said that all correspondence must be addressed to: "Alcaidia Ushuaia, Comisaria Ushuaia, Territorio Nacional de Tierra Del Fuego", or it would not be delivered. We passed the word along over the phone at the next opportunity, with the result that lots more telegrams arrived. But there were still very few letters. After a while I realised why letters were not getting through. The prison staff wanted the British stamps to keep as souvenirs. So I put it about that if any prison officer delivered a letter to me I would give him back the envelope and the stamp. Suddenly shoals of letters as well as telegrams began to arrive. They were from people I knew, and from people who had never met me. There were books and cassettes, and even specially commissioned cartoons from The Observer and the Sunday Times. There were letters from colleagues on The Observer and many other newspapers. David Blundy of the Sunday Times (later tragically shot dead in El Salvador) wrote a hilarious letter about the hacks gathered in Jerusalem to cover the Israeli invasion of south Lebanon. He described how Colin Smith, The Observer's chief foreign reporter, who had a military background but had missed out on the Falklands War, ran around the American Colony Hotel late at night with his arms flung out and making loud droning noises, pretending to be a Vulcan bomber. He almost bombed an armed Palestinian guard who did not see the funny side. School children wrote to us from all over the country, and their letters were always touching, often funny, although unintentionally so. One boy wrote: "I am very sorry that you can not be let free to see your family but I am sure you will. Buy (sic) the way I am not writing to talk about that. The other day I went on a trip and I went on the cork skrou but I don't think you will have heard of that but it's a carriage which go up-side-down on a track." Miss Berry, one of my primary school teachers from the World War II era decades earlier, wrote to say: "I still recall you and Tony (my brother) playing in the sand-pit at Deepdale Council School, and running into the shelters when the sirens went."

There was a sensitive letter from Richard Watson, a librarian who had worked with my mother in Preston Library for 30 years. During all those years he had never called her anything other than "Mrs. Mather". When I got back home I called him to ask if my mother had ever confided in him about her divorce from my father, which had happened when I was very young. He said that she had never mentioned it, and he had never asked. Several newspapers had the idea of encouraging their readers to write to us, and printed the address of the prison. The Lancashire Evening Post, published in my home town of Preston, was one such, and the gesture was well meant. Many of the letters were from religious people. Some were sweet. One woman wrote: "Spoken and silent prayers will be ascending to the Throne of Grace in great numbers....I am 75, and will now ride my cycle (pedal) to the G.P.O. to post this." Others brought back memories of an upbringing I had rejected. An elderly gentleman called George Crook wrote to me: "as a friend and your old Sunday School Superintendent at Carey Baptist Church and with the knowledge of your attendances at the Bible Study classes." He enclosed the chapel's latest news letter, containing the final pastoral letter of the Rev. Fred Wilson, who had married Margaret and me, and who was retiring after 37 years as pastor there. All these letters were well-meant, but the liberal use of quotations from the Bible and the promises of prayers for divine intercession somehow made me depressed. I would much have preferred a few anecdotes and the odd joke. However, I have to admit that I was moved by a letter from one hardened Fleet Street hack, who said he was surprising himself by praying for the three of us – adding almost apologetically: "At least it can't do any harm." I was particularly touched by all the family letters, especially from our children, Katie, then at New College, Oxford, Roderick doing his A levels, Juliet at Camden School for Girls, and, of course, lots of wonderful letters from Margaret, who somehow found cheerful things to say day after day.

As the days wore on tensions grew among the three of us, and our esprit de corps disintegrated. Differences emerged over what attitude we should take towards our captors. My view was that because of the strong feelings in the town, and indeed in the whole of Argentina, the prudent course would be to keep a low profile until the war was over in order to avoid drawing attention to ourselves. Simon felt it was important not to lose our identity in prison. Differences boiled down to ludicrous disagreements over things that simply did not matter. Every morning at 6 am we had to emerge from our cells and answer to a roll call. I answered "Presente" in Spanish, whereas Simon and Tony answered "Present" in English. My view remains that what I proposed was common sense not cowardice. After our release Simon described my attitude as "supine", and purported to have been the stiff upper lip Englishman. However, the image that stays in my mind is of him breaking down and bursting into tears. The only one of us to do so, he sat on his bed in the cell wailing: "I don't think we're ever going to get out of this alive, and I'll never see my family again." In the end, Simon decided to say "Presente" but did so with an exaggeratedly English public school accent, which caused hoots of laughter in the prison corridor and brightened up the day. Tony continued to shout "Present".

In early June Maria was released and as Rosa had been

transferred to a prison in Buenos Aires the women's section, with its two cells, became free, and the three of us were transferred to it. It was round the corner from the main corridor, and was separated by a metal gate. This meant that we did not have to take part in "Forma", and so could sleep longer. Also, from the window there was a fantastic view of Mount Olivia, a perfect snow-bound pyramid that dominates Ushuaia. At last we were also given knives. Yet to our amusement we found that all three of us continued eating with a piece of bread in one hand and a spoon in the other, as we had been doing for the previous two months. The downside was that we were now separated entirely from the other prisoners, and had to attract the attention of a prison guard if we wanted to go through to the main section. We slept in one cell, and used the other as a living room. We had enough money to buy a 9-inch colour TV, which we put in the other cell so I was able to escape to watch a lot of the World Cup that was taking place in Spain. But with no one but ourselves for company, relations deteriorated even further. There were rows over minor matters. On one occasion I picked up The Times crossword that Simon had half completed and filled in a clue, causing him to become demented. Things got so bad that I told Simon I was going to apply for solitary confinement. When news of this reached the Sunday Times office it caused great hilarity. Simon was not the most popular reporter among his colleagues. He was considered to be something of an editor's pet. He was not on the staff, and had a contract which said he could live in Oxford, and need not work from the office, though Harold Evans, the Sunday Times editor, had added the phrase "but an occasional visit would be very much appreciated". His journalistic career was marked by extraordinary coincidences, which did not endear him to his colleagues. A few years after our release he passed through Rio Grande airport again when working on another story, and astonishingly, according to his report, the naval officer who had arrested us walked past him again without recognising him. Later still when reporting the plight of Albanian refugees from Kosovo he discovered that the field in which the refugees were encamped happened to be the same one in which he, his wife, Judy and their family had put down their tartan blanket for a picnic during a touring holiday of Yugoslavia years before. Tony was largely unaffected by these tensions. It was almost as though the Antarctic winter had turned the prison into a dark room where he felt at home. He would announce: "I think I'll go and see if any of the lads are brewing up". He would then sit happily for hours with other prisoners in their cells, supping maté, and chatting to them. It did not seem to matter that they did not know what he was saying, nor that he could not understand them. He was the only one of us who seriously contemplated the idea of trying to escape. He would study the small barred window high up on the bathroom wall, through which someone had once escaped, according to the other prisoners. We never discovered if this was true. If it was, he would not have got very far. Barrozo once told us that there was no point in trying to escape. The road to the western half of Tierra Del Fuego, which was Chilean, petered out at the border, which was an arbitrary vertical line on a map. Anyone who crossed into Chile in winter would have died in the snow-bound mountain wilderness. But Tony was an East End boy, and as a young man had come into contact with people who were no strangers to prisons. He told me he had worked for the Krays, notorious twins who had ruled and terrorised the East End. One day, he had been instructed to take a Mercedes for a drive, and "give it a proper work-out" by driving it as hard as possible over as many bumps a possible. When he returned it he discovered that there was a man tied up in the boot. He had also worked with Lord Snowdon, the photographer married to Princess Margaret. His dark room was beneath the floor boards in their home, and from there he could hear their increasingly acrimonious rows as their marriage deteriorated. He said he knew before anyone that they were heading for a divorce.

The opposing sides of the propaganda war

CHAPTER SEVEN

SURRENDER

As the British troops advanced toward Port Stanley my thoughts turned increasingly to the implications for us of an Argentine defeat. I wanted the British to win, of course. But above all I wanted to survive. On Sunday May 30 I wrote: "My assessment of our situation now is that the worst case scenario involving British attacks on the Argentine mainland, including even on Ushuaia, looks extremely unlikely. The main personal threat to us now seems to be the possibility that the Argentines might take the loss of the islands very badly, and take their revenge on us. This could mean a heavy sentence by the court, or even worse, the breakdown of law and order, and the re-emergence of the death squads." Already, I had heard of a group in Ushuaia that called itself "Volunteers for the Liberation of the Malvinas" that had stoned the house of the Chilean consul and set fire to his car because Chile had refuelled a Royal Navy ship.

Simon and I had held long, obsessive talks about what might lie ahead for us, and I mentioned our concerns to Barrozo. Barrozo reacted forcefully. He stood at the top of the stairs which led up from the prison entrance, and pointed to a line of guns on a rack behind him. "If they come up these stairs"….and he swung his arms as though spraying an approaching mob with an automatic rifle. "If any harm comes to you"….he indicated with his hand that his throat would be cut. In other words, we were important international prisoners, and his job and possibly his life depended on keeping us alive. He added that Ushuaia was the best place for us to be, because the authorities knew everyone who arrived and left the island. In Buenos Aires, on the other hand, there were death squads, and not even the prisons were safe from them. There was a move afoot among the international press based in Buenos Aires to have us transferred to a prison in Argentina so that we could have regular visits, and a story even appeared in some British newspapers saying that we were about to be moved. I swiftly let it be known through Hugh O'Shaughnessy that none of us wanted to move, and asked him to tell the journalists in Buenos Aires that the lobbying for our transfer should stop. After that there was no more talk of our being transferred from Tierra Del Fuego. But we still did not know how long we would be in prison if, as seemed increasingly likely, we were found guilty. One day we managed to secure a talk with the judge, and asked him to tell us straight the worst thing that could happen to us. He quoted at us Article 223 of Argentina's Penal Code, which said that anyone who procured or illegally obtained secret political or military information concerning the security, the means of defence or the external relations of the nation would be liable to imprisonment for between two and eight years. The judge told us that if the sentence were three years we would serve eight months. If it were more than three years we would serve two years. The possibility of our innocence did not seem to have occurred to him. Strange as it may seem, I returned to the prison walking on air. Two years maximum! I could work in the local hospital, the Ushuaia Regional Hospital, under supervision, as some of the other prisoners did, which would have been fascinating. I could learn Spanish properly. There could be family visits from home. I would definitely settle for that. All these years later my perspective is still such that the idea of three months imprisonment seems trivial – as long as you know that you will then be free.

As the war continued to swing against Argentina, the nature of the government propaganda changed. The tone became softer, and the bulletins became more like those issued by the British. In the end, they were almost too frank, giving lengthy reasons for Argentine military failures that included support from the US, the economic might of the European Union etc etc until it seemed like it was plucky little Argentina against the rest of the world. A forthcoming visit by the Pope probably also contributed to the change of tone. We had high hopes that it would lead to some sort of gesture by Argentina that could set us free. The Pope, or HF (Holy Father) as John Whale, a religious expert on the Sunday Times, described him, had been briefed about us. HF duly arrived in Buenos Aires, and a petition signed by over 300 journalists calling for our release was handed to him. Great work by Isabel and Hugh! At the local level, George Marshall, the Euro-MP for North London phoned Margaret to say he was taking up our case at the European Parliament. Wally Fawkes (Cartoonist at The Observer, later Sunday Telegraph) and his jazz band gave a special concert at the Tufnell Park Hotel, with our pictures on the walls.

As the British continued to advance they captured so many Argentine troops that they could not cope with them. There was a risk that some would die of cold or starvation at night, as there was not enough food or shelter. So it was decided to return them to Argentina as quickly as possible. Pictures of hundreds of Argentine troops waving white flags began to appear regularly on television as unit after unit surrendered. The flags were beautifully made, and some even seemed to be made of silk. Where did they get them? Had the mothers of the young conscripts packed them in their bags when they left home, just in case? Or had they been issued to them by the Argentine army? Surely not. Nothing like that could ever happen with the British Army. On TV we watched as large numbers of repatriated prisoners arrived by ship at Puerto Argentino, the Argentine naval base near Bahia Bianca. We saw them race across an open space and into the arms of their families. It became a nightly event, and every time the subtitle was the same – "The Return of Our Heroes". Yet there we were still stuck in prison. "What about us?" we kept shouting at the TV screen. Surely, the British Government could hold on to some prisoners, and arrange to exchange them for us! An Argentine naval captain, Alfredo Astiz, who had been captured in South Georgia, was also released. As a member of an interrogation group based at the Naval Mechanics School in Buenos Aires, where some 5,000 prisoners had been held, tortured and murdered during the Dirty War, he was wanted by Sweden and France. When he was captured he asserted his right to refuse to answer any questions, and was eventually released under the Geneva Convention. We sent the details to the judge to try to make the point that if he could be released, why not us? And why had the British Government not proposed an exchange? Even now Aziz is still not in the clear. He has been condemned in absentia in France for the murder of two French nuns. In Argentina, despite an amnesty, his case has been reopened. Suddenly it was all over. The entire Argentine Army in the Falklands surrendered. In my diary I wrote: "Monday 14 June. Comisario Barrozo did not yet know the Argentines had surrendered. 'That's terrible,' he said, when I told him, once again quoting the BBC World Service to tell our captors what they had been prevented from knowing. 'On Saturday the Argentine boxing champion lost. Yesterday our football team lost in the World Cup. And today the Argentine Army loses!' ".

A wave of reaction engulfed me. I must have been much more tense than I realised, and now the reaction set in. I wrote in my diary: "Heard it confirmed on the BBC that a cease-fire had been agreed 'provided the honour of the Argentine forces is not compromised'. Turned away from the radio, which was perched on the window. Went into dark corner of bathroom, broke down and wept. Only time this has happened. Outside it was dark, and the snow had stopped. Nothing visible except solitary red light above radio tower near prison.". However, to my relief Argentine propaganda on TV was suddenly transformed for the better. I remember asking George, a prison interpreter, what would be the attitude towards the three of us if Argentina lost the war. He replied that either they would be out for revenge, or they would shrug it off and try to forget it. Fortunately, the latter happened. I was moved to see a new government-sponsored advertisement after the fighting had stopped. It showed a crowd murmuring gently in the Plaza de Mayo in Buenos Aires. The accompanying voice said that Argentines were united no matter what their ethnic origin. Then a list of all ethnic groups that made up modern Argentina scrolled up the screen. "Britannicos" was there in its correct alphabetical place and without any adverse comment.

After the surrender a fierce power struggle broke out within the Junta. Galtieri had wanted to continue fighting, and he blamed the Army leader, General Mario Menendez, newly-appointed military governor of the Falklands, for the defeat. Then news came through that Galtieri had fallen. Then that he had been replaced by a hard-liner, which was bad. I wrote: "Suddenly my fear returned. I had decided that there was now a reasonable chance of freedom and that I had better wash the brown sweater I had been wearing every day since our incarceration. Tonight Margaret is going to phone and I was going to sound cheerful. Now I don't know how I'll sound. Must keep control, and follow the motto that has seen me through many a crisis all over the world: never show fear." (underlined) Then I heard Cal on the BBC World Service. He said that the judge had gone to Rio Grande to re-interview some of the witnesses, including the pilot of the Tierra Del Fuegan Government plane. Things were looking good, but perhaps not so much for the pilot! Barrozo came to our cell. He said civilian flights would resume the following day even though Tierra Del Fuego was still a war zone. He said many people blamed Galtieri for the original mess and Menendez for the surrender – 14,000 soldiers should not have surrendered to 9,000 British. I knew this well enough as a Defence Correspondent. An attacking force normally needs a ratio of three to one in its favour. Another bizarre fact. It was revealed that all telex communications from the Falklands went through London. The Cable and Wireless operator in the Falklands had continued to send messages for the Argentines in the normal way without informing them of this fact! The phones had also worked normally, so that British troops were able to use telephone boxes to ask Falkland Islanders if there were any "Argies" around!

June 21. The shortest day, but one of the best. I wrote: "Willy and Isabel arrived (their plane from Buenos Aires having been commandeered the previous day). Lots of hugs and kisses. They had already been to see the judge, who seems to have made a complete volte face. He virtually pleaded with Willy to ask for bail and said he would grant it to us for 100 million each (15,000 = 1 US dollar). He said the de facto ceasefire had removed any danger to the state that we, the accused, might have presented. He made the extraordinary remark that he could no longer hold us as enemies of the state given the way the Army had behaved. He was very bitter about the failure of the Army and Galtieri." As a former naval officer he had nothing to say about the performance of the Navy. When asked by Isabel, who was preparing a story for the Sunday Times, how he felt, Simon came up with an inspired response: "Sobre la luna" – over the moon. However, to the bemusement of Isabel, and probably everybody else, the three of us were unanimous in expressing our reservations about accepting the bail on the terms it was offered. Now that the tide had turned we wanted to try to clear our names completely, and at the very least we wanted a guarantee that we could leave the country, and not merely move into a local address in Ushuaia where we could be forgotten and end up being kept there for a long time. I wrote: "Isabel must have thought us very ungrateful for not jumping at the idea of bail. Our basic point is that the re-evaluation of the evidence promised by the judge is due tomorrow, and that the judge should be forced to come to a definite decision about our guilt." I remember a rather baffled Isabel muttering: "You really have become institutionalised."

My diary continued: "Everybody here is furious with the Army, not with us. Grieco and Barrozo met Willy and Isabel at the airport and carried their bags. Grieco said that he had kept quiet long enough, but was prepared to do so no longer. Isabel and Willy came round at midday. They advised us strongly to take the chance of bail, and Willy said he would immediately make a further application for us to leave the country." In his office the judge delivered a homily to us, and as he proceeded it was clear that he was saying what we wanted to hear. Not only were we to be granted bail, but we were also to be permitted to leave the country, even though as far as the court was concerned, my address was to become the Canal Beagle Hotel,

Ushuaia. All that remained was for the bail money to be sent to Argentina and handed to the court. Willy was to fly to Buenos Aires and return with the money the following Monday. Then we would be free. In my diary I wrote: "We were photographed signing the bail papers. The judge left the room, turned and said: "I don't suppose I shall see you again. Never let it be said that the Argentines are bad losers, and that we take our revenge on non-combatants." He was right on one point and wrong on the other. His final words to us were dignified and gracious. But I did see him again. Ten years later I was to return to Argentina and meet him in very different circumstances.

The surrender made Grieco very emotional. Unlike the Army, he said, his beloved Marines had fought to the end and had been the last to surrender. British officers had shaken their hands and called them 'valiant'. "One thousand Ghurkha deads in front of their position!" he told me in his almost perfect English. This was a great exaggeration. Yet later when I visited the Falklands, and climbed Tumbledown Mountain, which overlooks Port Stanley, I saw from the wreckage of equipment that had belonged to the 5th Marine Infantry Battalion, some 50 of whom had been killed there, that there had been a serious battle. It is acknowledged by the British Army that the Argentine Marines put up stiff resistance, the only Argentine unit to do so.

The following day we were taken back to court to collect our documents – passports, credit cards, my contacts book etc. Raoul, the judge's assistant, said that they were receiving phone calls from Buenos Aires protesting about our being set free. This was a disturbing development as we had to pass through Buenos Aires. We would not be able to relax until we were actually out of the country. Meanwhile, we were allowed to read some of the court documents, and one that was pointed out to me, written by Captain Jose Vargas, Head of Naval Intelligence, said that we had known the difference between Daggers and Mirages, which was very slight. He was right about the difference between these two types of war planes being very slight. But I have no idea why he thought we knew what the differences were. I certainly didn't. But if details such as this got into the hands of the violent political elements that lurked beneath the surface in Argentina things could get very nasty for us.

As it became clear that it was only a matter of days before we were free the prison conditions were relaxed. I was allowed out (accompanied) to buy a warm jacket as I thought we might be taken all the way to Buenos Aires by car. The shop at first refused my American Express card as it had a London address. When I started to walk out of the shop, the assistants changed their minds. Back in the jail I wrote: "Sent birthday telegram to Katie. 'Happy Birthday. Save a piece of cake for me. It won't be stale. Love, Dad XXXXX', and typed it on an official telegram form. First time I have used a typewriter for over two months." Barrozo then offered to take us in his car to what he described as a "special police lunch". The idea was that we would meet some of his colleagues in a relaxed setting away from the prison. He loaded steaks and wine in cardboard boxes in the boot of his car, and we set off to a remote spot away from prying hostile eyes. Simon had also asked if there was any chance of our being taken to see some guanacos, Tierra Del Fuegan llamas that are smaller than those in mainland Argentina. Barrozo agreed. We drove about eleven miles through a military training area where most of the signs were pock-marked with bullet holes, until we came to a frozen lake (Lake Roca) near which was a hut that was used by the Marine Infantry. The first thing that happened was that when we got out of the car all three of us fell back on our backs. It was not just that it was slippery underfoot. The real reason was that for three months our eyes had become used to the interior walls of the prison, so could not focus on distances. We got up and staggered into the hut, which had badges on the walls, one of which said "Division Victor". There was a reddish brown animal skin nailed to the wall. Barrozo pointed to it, and announced proudly "Guanaco!" That was not exactly what Simon had had in mind! Barrozo had underestimated the animosity towards us in the town. A small group of heavily-clad Argentines was sitting in the hut. "Don't let them know you are prisoners," he whispered to us. "Say you are tourists."

"They're tourists", he announced in a loud voice. A tall man in a woolly hat approached me. "The Malvinas are Argentine!" he shouted in my face. They had recognised us from photographs in magazines and from TV, and our cover had lasted only a few seconds. Barrozo decided we could not stay there, and drove us back to the prison, with the steaks and wine still in the boot. By the time we got back we had missed our evening meal. So much for the special police lunch.

By now we had hoped we would be on our way home. The United Nations Secretary General, Perez de Cuellar, had announced our impending release. But there was a hiccup. We were stuck in prison because the bail money had not arrived. It turned out that The Observer Accounts Department had sent an inadequate sum of money to the wrong place. Surprise! Surprise! They had sent it to Thomas Cook's in New York instead of to Bob Chesshyre's (The Observer Washington Correspondent) account in Washington. The result was that we spent at least four more unnecessary days in prison. While we were waiting I wrote: "A very boring day, tense and difficult because we feel we should be on our way by now. A major-general has been arrested for criticising the handling of the Malvinas crisis by the military. It makes us even more anxious to get out of here."

The next day, Sunday, Grieco took us to meet Natalie Goodall, an American botanist, and author of "Tierra Del Fuego", now a classic book consisting of text and pen drawings of Tierra Del Fuegan wild life, reminiscent of Wainwright's Lake District books. After retreating with her Argentine husband to their estancia called Haberton, 85 kilometres from Ushuaia, for the duration of the war, she had returned to her wooden house in the centre of Ushuaia. She told us an interesting story. At the height of the fighting an Argentine naval helicopter had landed in a field near the farm house. Out stepped the admiral in charge of the southern region. He said he was making sure that Argentines with foreign connections were free from harassment. She told him she had experienced no problems. He handed her his visiting card, and told her to call him directly if she had any trouble. We stayed several hours chatting, drinking tea and looking at her collection of dolphin bones. She carried out research into dolphins, around 20 of which were washed up on the shore each year. She asked us if we would take some dolphins' teeth to a scientific research department at Cambridge because she was unsure about postal deliveries to the UK. In the fly leaf of a copy of her book, which I had bought when we first arrived in Ushuaia, I had written: "Ian Mather. Ushuaia Prison. Argentina. Arrived April 15 1982. Departed?" Now Natalie wrote: "Hoping that, in spite of it all, you will have nice memories of Tierra Del Fuego. Saludas, Natalie Goodall, Ushuaia, 27 June 1982." Grieco drove us back to the prison. He was pale, exhausted and still furious. He told us that the commander of the 5th Marine Battalion had struck Menendez on the chin for surrendering.

In the end, The Sunday Times, professional as ever, paid the bail money for all three of us. However, we were still concerned about potential threats in Buenos Aires because of the dark mood of bitterness now sweeping the country, and feared that it could be directed at us when we arrived there. I was unhappy about the general political situation in Argentina, and feared that we could be re-arrested by the military. So we asked Barrozo if we could hire a car and be given a safe conduct to head to Rio Grande and cross into Chilean Tierra Del Fuego from there so that we would remain under the jurisdiction of Judge Sagastume until we left the country. It was my idea, and news of it led Hugh and some others, including a BBC Newsnight team, to head for Punta Arenas to meet us. Barrozo agreed, and we went to see the Chilean consul in Ushuaia to ensure that there would be no problems at the border. On our way we walked past the Argentine warships moored in the port. Our prison minder laughed and made "glug glug" noises, indicating sinking ships. A week or so earlier he would never have dared do such a thing, but by now all respect for the military had evaporated. One last job was to donate our TV set to a local Roman Catholic orphanage in the town, and return to prison to pack our bags. But the judge was not finished with us yet. At 6.30pm we were called to his office. Once again he was not there to meet us, which was a bad sign. Willy was there. He told us the judge was angry because of our proposal to leave for Chile. Not only was Chile an unfriendly country, but it had given material support to Britain during the Falklands War. In its government announcements it even referred to the Falklands as the Falklands and not the Malvinas. Willy said the judge had thought of refusing us permission to leave. Instead, he now insisted that we should go directly to Buenos Aires, where we should hand in our press credentials. It was clear that his main concern was that there would be a backlash against him if it became known that the three British "spies" had ended up in Chile.

Barrozo then called us into his office and said he wanted to be sure we had no complaints. I mentioned being photographed naked on a bed. He was very concerned, and explained at length that the examination had been carried out by a doctor from the hospital to ensure that there had been no marks on us when we arrived from military custody. A prison officer whom we called "Hot Lips" because he had thick lips explained that in acting as one of our guards he had only been doing his job. He gave us a bottle of wine and asked for our autographs. He said: "You are the most important people I have ever met." We gave him some chest expanders that had been given to us. Other prison officers and prisoners signed their names inside the fly leaf of Natalie Goodall's book. So did Jane Scotti and Marghuerita Vasquez, to whom we said a fond farewell. There was no chance to say goodbye to Ullman. He had appeared in the door of the dining room with his head shaved. He said that this was because the Argentine boxing champion had lost, the Argentine football team had lost and the Argentine armed forces had lost. The next day he was taken to Buenos Aires for psychiatric treatment.

At around 10 pm we set off in two cars with a police escort, on a four-hour drive through the night along Ruta 3 to Rio Grande. There an Aerolineas Argentinas Boeing 727 was waiting with its engines running – just for us. It was now around 2.30 am, and our only company on the plane was a couple of Argentine passengers, who must have got wind of the special flight and obtained permission to get on it. Suddenly Grieco appeared in full Marine uniform. He stood stiffly

Journalists on their way home

Ian Mather (top) and his Observer colleague Tony Prime.

THE THREE British journalists held on spying charges in southern Argentina since April 13 were on their way home today.

Simon Winchester of the Sunday Times and Ian Mather and Tony Prime of the Observer were freed yesterday on bail of 100 million pesos each (around £50000) by the federal judge at Ushuaia, Enrique Sagastume, and told they could leave the country.

This morning the three men were reported to have travelled overland from the ice-bound town where they spent 17 days in jail to Rio

by Diane Chanteau

Gallego, where they boarded a flight for Buenos Aires.

They had been arrested by security police while photographing military installations near Rio Grande, north of Ushuaia.

Before leaving they told local reporters that they had been well treated during their detention.

Court sources were quoted as saying that the men had heaters in their cells as well as television sets and "three heavy meals a day".

Sunday Times editor Frank Giles said today he was hoping to see them back in

London "as soon as they can hop on a plane."

"We have never admitted and neither have they to being guilty of anything at all. So it is quite right and proper that they should not have to stand trial for something they did not do."

The three men always argued that they were engaged only in normal reporting when they were arrested.

In El Salvador, the abandoned vehicles of six journalists have been found on a road north of the capital San Salvador, apparently at the scene of a guerrilla attack on a bus. Among the missing is British cameraman Julian Harrison of United Press International.

Simon Winchester of the Sunday Times.

Periodistas liberados

USHUAIA (DYN). — Los tres periodistas británicos procesados aquí por espionaje recuperaron anoche su libertad, luego de que su abogado defensor, Carlos Balaban, depositó en el Banco Nación los 300 millones de pesos de fianza, pero el juez Federal de esta ciudad, doctor Enrique Sagastume, aún no los autorizó a abandonar la ciudad.

El juez dijo que a partir de este momento los tres periodistas, Ian Mather y Tony Prime, del "The Observer", y Simon Winchester, de "Sunday Times", quedaron en libertad dentro de la ciudad y que podrían pedir autorización especial para viajar al norte del país o al extranjero, lo que hizo el abogado defensor.

El abogado Balaban viajó a esta ciudad desde la Capital Federal, en un

vuelo de Líneas Aéreas del Estado (LADE), trayendo la suma fijada para la fianza, según el auto de excarcelación dictado por Sagastume el 23 de este mes.

Posteriormente, Balaban depositó el dinero en el banco y concurrió a entrevistar al juez.

British and Argentine news reports of the release
of the three British journalists

110

upright in the aisle just as he had done when we had first set eyes on him in the prison. He declared: "This was a war without hatred. But you know how strongly we feel about the Malvinas. We'll be back." We shook hands, he left, and we took off. We landed at Aeroparque at 7 am to find a press scrum waiting for us, and a Swiss diplomat called Daniel. We piled into his Mercedes, and set off at a cracking pace with the press in hot pursuit. For once in my life I had the experience of being chased by the press, and I must say I found it great fun as we ducked and dived through the Buenos Aires early morning traffic. Then as we were racing along a straight dual carriageway Daniel announced: "I am now going to do something which is very un-Swisslike." He hauled the car into a U-turn which took us across the central reservation, and off in the opposite direction, leaving the press cars way behind. At the British ambassador's residence, which was still occupied, we were given breakfast of orange juice and toast, but not a traditional English breakfast, for which I was drooling. I then rang Margaret, spoke to all the family, had my first bath for three months and went to sleep in a proper bed. Margaret told me that shortly after we had left she had rung the prison, and a prison officer had told her: "Libertad". It was a word she had waited a long time to hear.

In the evening we were taken to the airport for an overnight Iberia flight to Madrid. For the last time we were once again incarcerated "for our own protection", this time in a private lounge near the aircraft at Ezeiza Airport. At the last moment a young woman appeared with our passports, boarding cards and tickets. We were led on to the Iberia 747, shown to three separate first class seats, and the plane immediately took off. As the nose lifted off the ground we looked at each other, smiled and gave thumbs-up signs. We did not speak again on the flight, which I recall being very rough. We landed in Madrid to transfer to a British Airways flight. There a local British freelance journalist, whom I knew, had been enterprising enough to get to speak to us, and after a brief interview we were off again. This time we were on a BA flight full of British football supporters on their way home from a World Cup match. The captain announced to the

The family at the 1982 press conference
at Gatwick Airport

passengers that he particularly welcomed the three British journalists on their release from Argentina. Suddenly everybody wanted to shake our hands. Among them was the Minister for Sport, Neil Macfarlane, who came and talked to us. Glass after glass of champagne was thrust into my hands. All this after two nights without sleep on our way home. At Gatwick, our families were waiting. An official who dealt with stress cases appeared to check that we were up to meeting them, and then announced: "Your families are behind that door." A joyful reunion followed, and then a televised press conference, in which I appeared in a clean shirt but an old sweater much worn in prison. The next day my mother said to me: "Oh you did look tired!" Out of my mind with fatigue, reaction and champagne, in fact. At last I was home in Muswell Hill, where a big party had been organised. The next job was to write an account of my imprisonment for The Observer, based on my diary. For that I owed a huge debt to Trevor Grove, editor of The Review section where the article appeared. Simon was given a similar slot in the Sunday Times, in which he reported that he had continued to record the movements of military planes and ships that he had been able to observe through the cell window. This was very peculiar, given the fact we were still on bail. The news agencies picked up on it as the intro to their stories on our release. Shortly after that Margaret and I sat down and wrote many thank you letters. Then we took the family on a long break to Sri Lanka, Hong Kong and China. As for the other two, I remain good friends with Tony, who has returned to Britain after spending some years in France running a guest house with Hilary. Simon is a successful author.

Poder Judicial de la Nación

STS 826/8

///huaia, 11 de octubre de 1.988.-

AUTOS Y VISTOS:

RESUELVO:

DECLARAR EXTINGUIDA POR PRESCRIPCION LA ACCION
PENAL en la presente causa N° 8.339, y consecuentemente, SOBRESEER DEFINI
TIVAMENTE en la misma y respecto de IAN JAMES MATHER, de conformidad con
lo estatuído en los arts. 443 inc. 8° y 454 del Cód. de Proc. en Mat. Penal.-

Notifíquese, regístrese, y oportunamente comu-
níquese.-

zf*

OSCAR ENRIQUE SERANTES PEÑA

Ante mí:

NATIONAL JUDICIAL AUTHORITY

Ushuaia [?], 11 October 1988.

PROCEEDINGS
To order that criminal proceedings in Case No 8,339 should be
time-barred.

I HEREBY RESOLVE:

TO DECLARE THE CRIMINAL ACTION in Case 8,339 TIME-BARRED, and
in consequence, TO STAY PROCEEDINGS DEFINITIVELY in that case
concerning IAN JAMES MATHER [SIMON ADRIAN BERNARD WINCHESTER]
[ANTHONY ROBERT PRIME] in accordance with the provisions
of Article 443 (8) and Article 454 of the Code of Criminal

Ushuaia court documents declaring the case time-barred

CHAPTER EIGHT
BACK TO ARGENTINA

But was it really over? Back in Argentina the case rumbled on. From time to time a telex message would arrive from the court in Ushuaia to say there would be a hearing to announce a verdict. I insisted on replying that I wanted no verdict to be given in my absence, and that I must be allowed time to travel to Ushuaia to appear. Some people thought I was mad. Anthony Whittaker, the Sunday Times lawyer, in an internal memo described me as an "imbecile". However, I stuck to my belief that the Argentines would be unwilling to confront us face-to-face, and the ploy worked. They backed away every time. At one point, two years after I returned home the Argentine court declared me (and I think the two others) a "fugitive from justice". There had been a failure to apply to renew our bail, which had to be done on a regular basis, because Willy Balaban was no longer involved in our case. He had withdrawn as the result of a dispute over money. I immediately wrote to the court to explain the situation. I wrote: "I wish to state that, while maintaining my innocence, I remain entirely willing to abide by the rules of the Argentine judicial process. I would like to continue to remain on bail until this matter is settled as I am working as a journalist with The Observer and am with my family. However, if it is your wish that I should return to Ushuaia I remain willing to do so, as this is a clear legal and moral obligation." I knew perfectly well that the last thing the court in Ushuaia wanted was the reappearance of any of the three British journalists. What they wanted was to be able to catch us out by claiming that we had jumped bail, and then declare us guilty. My letter put a stop to it.

The court never did come to a verdict. After seven years the case ran out of time under the Statute of Limitations, and a new judge who had taken over from Sagastume declared the case "extinguished". We ended up neither guilty nor innocent, an honourable draw, I would say. The episode confirmed my low opinion of the Sunday Times lawyer. Despite a career in law he failed to understand or chose to ignore the burning sense of injustice that motivates an innocent person to try to clear their name. He also chose to ignore the fact that the three of us had direct experience of the Argentine system, and had seen at first hand the fear of court officials in Ushuaia of any personal confrontation with us.

Eventually, I did get to experience the natural beauty of Tierra Del Fuego. I returned to Argentina three times in 1991 ahead of the tenth anniversary of the Falklands War to make a documentary for the BBC. My first visit was to do the research and find out what sort of reception I could expect. Then when it was clear that there would be no animosity I returned with a film crew to do the filming. Finally, using the money from the BBC I went on holiday there with Margaret. By 1991 the Falklands War had receded into the background as far as most Argentines were concerned. On the road from the airport into Buenos Aires there was one sign that said: "The Malvinas are Argentine." But I saw no others. During one of my visits for the BBC programme I happened to be in Buenos Aires on June 14, the anniversary of the Argentine surrender. It had been designated "Treason Day", to point the blame at the Junta, now long since gone from the political scene. But hardly anyone turned up in the Plaza de Mayo, and the then President, Carlos Menem, himself had set an example by declaring that he was going skiing.

I landed at Rio Grande on the way to Ushuaia to find that the airport where I had been arrested was quiet. There were no longer any military jets taking off and landing, and the bunkers round the perimeter were abandoned and overgrown. But Ushuaia was very much as I had remembered it. It was deep in snow as we were filming in June, the same time of the year that I had been there. Each morning the tourist office put a sign in its window which said whether or not the only road out, Road Number 3 to Rio Grande, was "transitable" or "intransitable" because of the snow. While I was there the locals celebrated the shortest day with the Festival of the Longest Night. There was a big parade, and in the evening people skied down the mountainside carrying flaming torches, and danced and drank beer and hot chocolate until midnight. I asked for a room with a view of the prison rather than of the Beagle Channel, which must have seemed a strange request. I got what I wanted, Room 324, and spent a lot of time sitting in the window, staring at the prison and preparing my questions for the interviews. The conditions were hard especially for the film crew, as it was bitterly cold and slippery. At times my beard froze. The sound recordist, Abalardo Kushnir, from Buenos Aires, became a laughing stock for the number of times he fell flat on his back. But I was delighted to learn five years later that his career had blossomed and that an Argentine film on which he did the sound recording, called The Official History, won a Hollywood Oscar for the Best Foreign Film. I walked by myself up to the prison. It was snowing hard as I went round the back and looked up at the row of barred windows from which I had looked down at the electricity pumping station, now a ruin. I detected a movement. Then a hand appeared. I waved, and the hand waved back. I went round the side to where the kitchen was, and heard knocking on the windows from the inside. Once again I waved, and once again I saw the outlines of hands waving back. Once again, I felt a swell of sympathy for the people inside. During the night I was awakened by loud crashing noises that I had forgotten all about. It was the sound of chunks of ice falling off roofs. Ushuaia is the only place in the world I know where it seems to freeze and thaw at the same time.

We did most of the outdoor filming first as we wanted moody shots in blizzards. As I was being filmed taking a photograph of the Argentine naval base an Argentine sailor with a rifle emerged and marched up to us. I felt a frisson of anxiety at the thought of history repeating itself. Suddenly he fell flat on his back after slipping on the ice, and when he had pulled himself up he merely said "Privado" – private. We apologised and he walked away. I was then filmed looking at the prison through binoculars and making notes in a local restaurant beneath a whale bone and an animal skin nailed to the wall.

By the time of my return to Argentina in 1991 a curse seemed to have struck many of those who had acted against us. The Fiscal had died, as had Raoul, the judge's assistant, who had drowned in a local lake. The judge had had a serious operation. Many of the men who had held absolute power over life and death had fallen from favour. A democratically-elected government had replaced the Junta, and had proceeded to take revenge on the armed forces for having led Argentina to humiliation. Grieco had not only lost his fine wooden house that stood on a spur of land protruding into the Beagle Channel. He had been expelled from the Navy and sent to prison for embezzlement. He told me that when he re-emerged from prison he had gone to Buenos Aires and tried his hand as a detergent salesman, but had decided to return to the more sheltered environment of Ushuaia after one of his daughters became pregnant by a street artist. He was now seeking to rebuild his life by working as a freelance tour guide. He was hoping to be part of an Argentine company that arranged for tourists, mostly American, to travel from Ushuaia to the Falklands and then on to Antarctica. The company's promotional literature called Port Stanley, "Puerto Stanley" instead of the Argentine name, Puerto Argentino, which few foreign tourists would have recognised. Grieco said he had taken exams, but had got only six out of ten. He had not even been able to afford a phone. He pointed to a gap in his front teeth and said it would cost 2,000 dollars to fix it, but he showed no visible signs of resentment at his loss of status. He even joked about the fact that he had just been able to buy a cheap Russian car, claiming that he could park anywhere in town since it had no number plates. But he hated the domestic role. As we sat in his kitchen he donned an apron, self-mockingly hung his head and said: "Me macho!" He told me that the night before the General Belgrano sailed from Ushuaia some of the officers had been at his

*With Marine Commander Juan Carlos Grieco,
now a tour guide*

house, and had made phone calls home. For some they were the last phone calls they would ever make. The following morning a sailor had arrived with an ash tray inscribed with the name of the General Belgrano as a gift from them. He showed me the ashtray and proudly declared: "This is the last public relations ashtray from the General Belgrano". He also produced a piece of varnished wood from the deck of the General Belgrano, which had been given to him by an officer when he had attended the arrival in Ushuaia of the dead and wounded in a hospital ship. He said he had seen a lifeboat full of sailors all frozen to death. On the roof was a sailor holding a light, also frozen to death. In a bizarre reversal of roles I was able to hire Grieco for the documentary as a tour guide to show me the town I had glimpsed through prison bars and the surrounding countryside. He remained bitterly disappointed at the loss of the Malvinas. "The

Malvinas are under our skin," he said. "It's like a son whom you cannot reach. He is still your son." On a more mundane level he told me that after we had been arrested our rooms had been searched by "Barrozo's men", and that I had left behind "a pair of socks that smelt".

Admiral Zaratiegui, who had been in charge of the Southern Region of the Navy, had also lost his job. A hard-line militarist, he had refused to stand up in the presence of Raoul Alfonsin, Argentina's civilian president, who had come to power in a democratic election after the Falklands fiasco, and had even issued a statement saying that Alfonsin had no moral authority. Grieco had supported Zaratiegui's stance, and that could have been the real cause of his undoing. Zaratiegui had been sent to prison, and when I returned to Argentina had a new career as first officer on a cruise ship that sailed along the Paraguay River. I interviewed him in Buenos Aires. Self-mockingly, he produced a visiting card describing his occupation as "former prisoner". He was very bitter over the Falklands. It transpired that he had been kept in the dark about the plan to invade after falling-out with the Junta. This was despite his seniority and the fact that he had taken a naval staff course at Greenwich and so had some understanding of the how the Royal Navy functioned. I asked him if he was angry. "Yes," he replied in English, dispensing with the interpreter. "Angry!" Zaratiegui died in 2002, still an embittered man.

The fate of Grieco and Zaratiegui mirrored that of the armed forces in general. The public reaction to the humiliation was so intense that former officers did not dare show themselves in the street. The Navy declined into a lamentable state, starved of funds, its ships permanently tied up. Pay was so low that even officers were forced to take a second job. Military buildings in Buenos Aires closed at midday as there was no money for electricity, and every other taxi driver in Buenos Aires seemed to be a moonlighting military person. In Ushuaia the local council laid out a "Malvinas Park" in which there were plaques honouring the Argentine fallen. Yet when I went it was unvisited and the lawn overgrown and full of dandelions. I also visited

Judge Sagastume at his apartment in Bahia Bianca near Buenos Aires. He was now retired and recovering from a serious operation on his face, I asked him if he had thought that I had been a spy. He replied that probably not, but that that had not been the issue. The question had been whether we had seen things that could have been of use to the British military. He had not been willing to take the risk. That seemed a fair enough answer to me.

Barrozo, on the other hand, was prospering. As a civilian detective who had trained for six years at the Buenos Aires police academy, he was untainted by the Argentine humiliation in the Falklands. I was pleased for him because I had the highest regard for his professionalism. Barrozo appeared delighted at the reappearance of one of his most notorious charges. He insisted on giving me a lift from the prison to the hotel in his car even though the distance was only 100 yards or so. The reason became clear when we took off in the opposite direction. Barrozo took the most circuitous route possible, driving down the middle of the road and tooting his horn and pointing at me whenever he passed anyone he knew, which appeared to be half the town. It was as though he was conveying royalty. After the overthrow of the Junta and the sacking of Grieco he had become chief of police and had inherited the chief's splendid official residence. Grieco moved literally across the street, where through the lace curtains of his modest bungalow he had the galling experience of seeing his former home stand empty because Barrozo did not move in. "I had my own personal house," Barrozo told me. "So I used the official house only for public relations and official dinners." Barrozo eventually retired early from the prison service. He was able to do so, he said, because Tierra Del Fuego was a hardship posting, and each year of service counted double. We filmed at Barrozo's house, where his wife cooked dolce de latte pancakes. They had remembered that in prison I had expressed a fondness for the stuff, which was basically condensed milk. He had a large collection of yerba maté bowls, and a dog called Richard. He produced the biggest bottle of whisky I have ever seen, and after the filming we all

With former prison governor Jose Barrozo

In the prison dining room in 1991

got drunk. Barrozo was now also an estate agent and owned several "personal houses". He was a theatrical impresario too, and President of the local Rotary Club, which he regarded as a great honour. The Rotary Club gave a dinner for me in a private room in a restaurant called The Blue Room in San Martin. This is the Oxford Street of Ushuaia, the main difference apart from the fact that San Martin is short and narrow, is that every shop of whatever type has collections of bottles of whisky and cigarettes in the window. Barrozo and I made speeches. Barrozo said it was an appropriate day because in Argentina it was the National Day for Journalists, and read out a long list of greetings to journalists from local companies and individual citizens, plus a homily from a local priest on the virtues of journalism. What a contrast with my visit in 1982. I replied jokingly that I hoped there would be a National Day for Spies so that I could return for another equally convivial event.

I also discovered that Maria, the woman from the Igloo night club, had built herself a new life. I knocked on the door of the house in which she was now living in the hope that she would agree to be in the film. She was astonished to see me, then delighted, then worried. It was the middle of the day, and she explained that she was now married to a bank manager, who was at work. He did not know about her previous career, and she did not want him to find out. They had an 11-year-old son. She had bought their house with her own money, and a car. I said words to the effect that her secret was safe with me, wished her well, and said I would never trouble her again. I still wish her well, and hope her past never returns to haunt her.

Barrozo used his influence to enable me to revisit the prison, where we were allowed to film. Near the entrance was a cleaning duty roster which I remembered. But there was a new painting showing the roads to heaven and hell. The former was narrow and winding and ran past churches and Biblical texts. The latter was broad and lined with casinos and bars. He pulled the old prison records out of a drawer, and showed me where I had signed my name on being admitted, and given the prison number 544. My biggest surprise was the discovery that my old cell was now occupied by a young woman with a baby. Little Dario – named rather surprisingly after a Nicaraguan poet - was sleeping peacefully in his cot. A makeshift clothes line festooned with nappies completed what could have been a typical domestic scene, were it not for the rusty iron bars across the window that I knew so well. Sandra, the baby's mother, greeted me with the desperately affectionate embrace of one whose life lacked a safe anchorage. That week an Argentine court had sentenced her to 25 years in prison for double murder. She was 24 years old and would serve at least 17 years. She and two men, one of them her husband, had been stealing cattle when they were recognised by two farmers. They shot the farmers dead and fled in a van. However, the police matched the tyre marks at the scene of the crime with the tyres on the van. The two men had been given life sentences. Sandra's husband had died apparently of asthma shortly before my visit. I met the other man in his cell a few yards away separated by a barred gate. A bulky figure with long hair, he was whiling away his days making model sailing ships out of Marlborough cigarette packets. The baby had been conceived after Sandra's arrest and detention. The prison authorities said they did not know who the father was, and Sandra was not telling. She had been allowed out of prison from time to time in the company of a woman prison officer, who also denied any knowledge. The court's verdict meant that Sandra would be sent to a women's prison, and Dario taken from her and adopted. There was another bleak coincidence. Sandra was the daughter of Rosa, the severely damaged woman who had murdered her 13th child, whom I had met ten years earlier in the prison.

None of the prisoners I had known were now in the prison. But the prisoners who were there agreed to be filmed. They stood at the entrances to their cells as the camera moved along the corridor, muttering to each other to avoid looking at the camera. On the prison TV there was an advertisement for yerba maté, and another which said: "Animal diarrhoea shortens life". Definitely preferable to the endlessly repeated "Vamos Argentinos. Vamos a Vencer", to which

I had been subjected. I bought a tree made from pieces of copper from one of the prisoners. Another asked me if I had been beaten up. A third said he himself had been. Barrozo, who accompanied us along the corridor, said the prisoners could get up whenever they liked in the mornings. Behind his back the prisoners shook their heads at this. All 30 or so of the prisoners I had known had either been released or transferred, and trying to find even those who were still in Tierra Del Fuego had proved a frustrating experience. The Tierra Del Fuegan police, who had always assured me that nothing moved on the island without their knowing about it, had confidently promised they would place their entire resources at my disposal to track them down. While we were filming in the prison a police officer came up to me and told me they had set up a special police squad to find the former prisoners. However, the ex-criminals thought that they must be in trouble if the police were looking for them, so had gone to ground. In the end the police did manage to track down one former prisoner. But when I met him I could hardly remember him, and he was extremely nervous. He was greatly relieved when the interview ended. It produced nothing of any use.

Peter Bate, the producer, and I went to see the judge who had taken over in Ushuaia. Under Argentine law I was supposed to be allowed to have my entire file now that the case had been terminated, and had indeed been promised it. Behind the judge's desk my foot-high file sat on a shelf. She took it down and started to read it. Something about the number of troops I had seen at Rio Grande waiting to be airlifted to the Falklands, and some details about Super Etendards. "Hm! Very interesting. You were very important. Your bail money was double that of the others because of your connections with the British War Ministry". Then she looked up and said: "I have decided not to let you have the file after all." We walked back to our hotel. There was silence. I said: "Right, come on out with it. You think I was spying, don't you?" Peter came out with an unconvincing denial. Silence again. We then went into the local bank unannounced, where we caused as much consternation as a hold-up. I asked to see the manager and demanded my bail money back. After many mutterings and much to-ing and fro-ing they declared that because of inflation over ten years the 7,000 dollars in Argentine pesos was now worth 10 dollars. I told them that the judge had told us that he had given instructions for the bail money to be kept in dollars not pesos. They searched again, and said they could find no such authority. So I gave up. Someone did well out of us. But it was a bit of fun.

Back in Buenos Aires I went to see an Argentine human rights lawyer, Luis Moreno Ocampo. He explained on camera that the most important event from the moment for our survival was when we were given individual prison numbers. That guaranteed that we could not become Dirty War victims, most of whom had never been found since they had never been officially registered. Moreno was one of a legal team set up to prosecute Argentina's generals and admirals responsible for torture and murder. In 2003 he was to become the first Chief Prosecutor of the International Criminal Court in The Hague, which he still is at the time of writing. When filming was complete Gabriel, our Argentine fixer, invited us all to lunch at his farm. "I tell Gomez keel (his pronunciation) a small cow", he said. Gomez was the farm hand, and the young cow, which we ate the next day, was delicious. Our final gathering was for dinner in a Buenos Aires restaurant. Carmen, our interpreter, had struck up a relationship with one of the BBC crew, and was due to go with him on the overnight ferry across the River Plate to Montevideo for the weekend, but was hesitating. "Go, and think of the Malvinas, Carmen", Gabriel roared. The two of them left.

Later in the same year I went for the third time to Argentina, this time using the money from the BBC to show Margaret "the scene of the crime". We headed straight for Ushuaia. Margaret wrote an article that was published in The Times to coincide with the showing of the documentary. In it she wrote that on our first evening in Ushuaia as we strolled along the waterfront she found it impossible not to be moved by the simple monument to the General Belgrano, which the municipality had erected. It stood on a promontory facing east

Memorial to the General Belgrano dead in an Ushuaia park

towards the Falklands, the direction on which the General Belgrano had sailed on its final fateful journey. It took the form of a jagged grey piece of metal representing the cruiser's bows plunging into the sea encircled by a submarine's periscope sights. I think there is a new memorial there now.

Margaret's first encounter with one of my captors took place in bizarre circumstances. We had headed first to the local tourist office, where I had heard Grieco was to be found, and immediately we entered I heard his familiar voice in a back room, where he was making arrangements for a group of foreign tourists. I had not seen him since 1981, and he had no idea we were coming. He looked up in astonishment. I introduced Margaret. Immediately she asked: "Are you the person who kept my husband in prison for three months?" Hugely embarrassed, he stared at the ground and muttered some defensive remarks about it having been the decision of another naval intelligence officer whose name was new to me and also of the judge. "Pity", Margaret replied jokingly. "Because I was going to ask you: 'Why didn't you keep him longer?'" Not being used to the British sense of humour he was at a loss for words. However, he recovered, and drove us to the modest bungalow in which he now lived where he and his wife, Chichita, did bed and breakfast for ten dollars a night. I met Chichita, again, and learned that she had taken a teaching job to supplement her husband's small pension. As the wife of a former senior naval officer, she too had felt the effects of the popular revulsion against Argentine military rule.

As Grieco now had no authority our best chance of getting Margaret into the prison lay with Barrozo, and soon we were walking up the hill to the prison, where the governor was waiting to greet us. In The Times Margaret wrote: "It was a not unpleasant building with white-washed walls, which doubled up as the local police station. Only the bars on the upper floor gave a clue as to its function. This building had been the focal point of so much agony during the Falklands conflict. I had phoned it regularly after the Swiss Government had negotiated permission for me to speak to Ian once a week at midnight

British time on Thursdays. I entered the foyer, which was lined with photographs of former police chiefs, and climbed the stairs to the first floor. I was taken through a heavy iron gate, and there was an ominous rattle of chains as it was firmly slammed behind me. The prison itself is tiny, consisting of a corridor with a dozen or so cells along one side, and a couple of communal rooms on the other. The corridor was dark because the prisoners had draped thick blankets over their barred cell doors to provide themselves with some privacy, and there was no other light source apart from the cell windows. But it seemed a comfortable enough place, and was well-heated against the freezing outside temperatures. I had been inside the jail for no more than a few minutes when I found myself surrounded by prisoners trying to sell me their hand-made wares. While some cells were Spartan others were centres of cottage industries, with sellotape, glue, pencil, paper, old cigarette boxes and glossy pages from magazines strewn around. The glossy paper was for rolling into tight lengths to form 'building blocks' to be crafted patiently into all sorts of objects, some quite beautiful. I bought an exquisitely delicate paper model sailing ship for 20 dollars to take back to England. Another prisoner demonstrated to me a moving lampshade he had made from paper. The heat from a lighted bulb caused the paper shade to rotate slowly and gracefully. In the tiny prison cell the effect was almost hypnotic. The prisoner, a man in his thirties, told me he had been taught the trick by a previous prisoner, who in turn had learned it from another prisoner who had left. We were approached by a prison officer who remembered Ian, a man in his late thirties with a swarthy complexion. He was still doing the same job. When we asked why had not been promoted, he pointed to his swarthy features, and said: "Indio" – Indian.

"As during the time of Ian's imprisonment most of the prisoners were petty criminals, but I was told that there were also two murderers, a man and a woman, who had killed two farmers while trying to steal cattle. The woman was out of the prison apparently attending a class. It turned out to be Sandra, mother of Dario, whom Ian had met earlier in the year. Dario had now been adopted. Her partner in crime,

Margaret and photographs of former prison governors at Ushuaia prison in 1991

a large man in shorts, produced a fluffy substance which he indicated was for stuffing the pillows which a group of them were making. On some of the pillows they had embroidered the words: "Home Sweet Home". I asked to see the prison communications room to which Ian had been taken to talk to me on the phone. But the room had been completely demolished. I expressed my disappointment to the prison governor over coffee. He whispered something to one of his subordinates. A few minutes later the man reappeared carrying an old wooden switchboard, and placed it on the table in front of me. The instrument, which he had retrieved from the prison store, had provided the only direct means of communication between us during Ian's imprisonment. 'Souvenir. Souvenir', he joked. Suddenly 1982 seemed like only yesterday."

Barrozo was still a concert impresario, and had hired a local school gymnasium for a concert by Ignacio Guaranin, Argentina's leading folk singer. He invited Margaret and me to attend. Several hundred people, mostly of mixed Indian blood, sat in anoraks and fur coats, as the hall was unheated. They were drinking white wine and eating empanadas, Argentine versions of Cornish pasties only smaller and with more varied contents. Ignacio turned out to be a figure of Falstaffian proportions, who soon had the audience in raptures as he ran through his favourite songs, pausing from time to time to hold his very large guitar out horizontally so that he could use it as a shield to refresh himself from a plastic beaker of wine hidden behind a loudspeaker. Barrozo had found us two of the best seats, and produced a couple of bottles of white wine. He then strategically placed himself at the front of the hall to one side of the stage, from where he systematically swept the audience with his eyes, like a security man guarding a head of state. Though he was a vain man he was compassionate. His lengthy service in the police force had given him an insight into why people become criminals, and I never once heard him condemn a criminal. Many former prisoners sought his help. The local branch of the Rotary Club of which he was president, held regular dinners at which members agreed on small acts of charity, such as buying pairs of spectacles for poor people in Ushuaia, for which they paid out of their own pockets. Barrozo also belonged to Alfonsin's leftist Radical Party, and was one of the few Argentines who would admit openly that the invasion of the Falklands had been the wrong way to pursue Argentina's claim because of the suffering it had caused. In the street he pointed out a "Malvinas survivor", who, he said, had been wounded and "driven crazy temporarily". Now he was better, and owned a local cake shop. Barrozo invited us to meet his wife, Graziella, a registrar of births, marriages and deaths, and later took us to his "cabanita", a country cottage he was having built near a lake. As we drove 70 miles from Ushuaia through magnificent snow-covered mountains we passed many dams of twigs and logs which had been constructed across streams. Each time Barrozo jabbed his finger in their direction and bellowed "Castor!" (beaver) in the special loud voice he used for addressing foreigners. He explained that beavers had been introduced into Tierra Del Fuego from Canada by the Argentine Navy for hunting, and were now out of control. Our route took us along the floors of valleys in which were enormous peat

131

Margaret and local hunter, near Ushuaia

Reflecting on his war behind bars: Ian Mather (9.30pm)

9.30 War Stories: Defence Correspondent Ian Mather
● CHOICE: Sent by his newspaper to cover the Falklands invasion, defence correspondent Ian Mather got no further than Argentina where he was arrested on suspicion of spying and spent 81 days in prison. Instead of reporting news, he helped to make it. Returning to the scene of his incarceration for the first time, Mather chats amiably to his former adversaries who still seem unable to admit that there was no case against him. All is unfair in war. Unlike many of his colleagues, Mather is reluctant to condemn the Ministry of Defence disinformation which convinced the Argentines that no British landing was imminent. He reckons it shortened the war and may have saved his life. Among footage from 1982 is a reminder of Ian McDonald, the defence ministry spokesman, whose deadpan statements made him an unlikely media star. (Ceefax) (897426)

The Times TV guide

132

bogs. The peat was exported to Scotland for making whisky, he said. In Ushuaia itself there were indications that trade between Britain and Argentina had returned. During the Falklands conflict Cadbury's milk chocolate had disappeared from Ushuaia's duty-free shops to be replaced by German and Swiss chocolate, and whisky had turned into German champagne. But Scotch whisky was back, and every shop, no matter what else it sold, had a display of bottles. Barrozo's cabanita turned out to be a small triangular hut made from lengua trees, a common species in Tierra Del Fuego. "It takes three trees to make one cabanita," he said. He ran around the perimeter of the small garden watering the rose bushes and pine trees he had just planted. The cabin smelt of fresh wood, and was in the process of being equipped with electricity and water. A large TV satellite dish had been erected at the end of the road. At the weekends Barrozo took his children fishing on the lake. Tierra Del Fuego had the biggest trout in the world, he said, along with Canada. But he worried about the education of his two children, a boy of 15 and a girl of 13. He liked Ushuaia because it was "familial". But the local university had courses only in tourism and commerce. On the other hand, he thought it was safer for his children than the north. Yet he seemed a happy man. He and Graziella insisted on driving Margaret and me to the airport to say goodbye. It was here that I had first met him when I had been handed to his custody by the Navy after being flown from Buenos Aires. It seemed a fitting farewell.

The documentary was shown on BBC2 on March 19 1992, the second of a four-part series on personal stories about the Falklands War. A number of newspapers gave it the accolade of "pick of the day". But any ego I might have had was quickly deflated. The Daily Mail's TV guide included an official prison photo of me holding a piece of card with my name on it. The writing was too faint to see. But at The European newspaper, where I was now working, an office wag filled in the space with the words "I work for The European. Please help me. Wife and eight kids" and stuck it on the office notice board. My third visit to Argentina, with Margaret, came immediately after the death of Robert Maxwell, the paper's owner, who drowned in mysterious circumstances when on his yacht near the Canary Islands. James McManus, the news editor, wanted me to cancel my holiday to fly to Jerusalem to cover Maxwell's burial on the Mount of Olives. But he gave up when I explained where I was going and what I had already spent in advance on the holiday. So another reporter was sent instead. Three weeks later the first thing I did when we landed at Madrid airport on our way home was to look for The European in the airport newsagents. To my relief it was still on sale. But the crash had only been delayed. It was taking time for Maxwell's convoluted financial affairs to be unravelled, and the disastrous state of affairs revealed. The day after my return Maxwell's empire crashed, and with it went my job without notice or compensation, and most of my pension. But that is another story. At the time it seemed relatively innocuous compared to what had happened to me in Argentina.

BIOGRAPHY

Ian Mather has been a journalist for 48 years, most of the time as a foreign and defence correspondent for national newspapers. After starting as a trainee reporter with the Press Association he moved to The Sun (before it was bought by Rupert Murdoch), the Daily Mail, and then for the biggest part of his career to The Observer, where he became Defence Correspondent and a foreign correspondent. He joined the now-defunct European newspaper as Diplomatic Editor. Starting with the British withdrawal from Aden he has reported from many conflict zones, including Vietnam, the Nigerian civil war, the Soviet invasion of Czechoslovakia, the Indo-Pakistan war, the Yom Kippur war, the Soviet invasion of Afghanistan, the Iran-Iraq War, the Gulf War and the conflicts in the Balkans. As a Diplomatic Editor, he also reported on numerous international news events, including major summits. He is now a freelance journalist and an international election monitor. He is married with three grown-up children and lives in Muswell Hill, London.